MICHAEL HAMBURGER

SELECTED POEMS

CARCANET

First published in 1988 by
Carcanet Press Limited
208-212 Corn Exchange Buildings
Manchester M4 3BQ

British Library Cataloguing in Publication Data

Hamburger, Michael
    Selected poems.
    I. Title
    821'.914

    ISBN 0-85635-752-9

The publisher acknowledges financial assistance
from the Arts Council of Great Britain

Typeset in 10pt Palatino by Bryan Williamson, Manchester
Printed in England by SRP Ltd, Exeter

Contents

7

Author's Note

Because I shirked the responsibility of making this selection, there is little I can or need to say about it beyond acknowledging the help of those who generously relieved me of a task I did not feel competent to take on. The selection was made by proportional representation – by a collation, virtually statistical, of the lists of chosen titles given to me by Jonathan Barker, Rosalind Belben, Anne Beresford and Richard Hamburger: two women, two men, two friends, two close relatives, a devoted reader, critic and librarian of contemporary poetry, a novelist and playwright, a fellow poet who is also my wife, and another who has chosen to take an interest in my work in spite of being my son.

No such resort or experiment was needed for my *Collected Poems* of 1984 and 1985, since it included all the poems I had passed for publication to date, other than those early ones I could no longer recognize as mine. Apart from that vexed matter of my juvenilia, there was no call on me to discriminate between one poem and another, only to confirm my responsibility for them all, regardless of my personal, almost certainly eccentric, preferences. It is these that would have prevailed in any selection made on my own – to the detriment, once more, of my earlier verse, and with an irresistible bias towards the more recent, only because it is closer to my present concerns.

If this selection is a balanced one, as I think it is, I have my four selectors to thank for that. (I should never have opened it with a poem written at the age of seventeen, but that poem was chosen unanimously, with four votes, and I have never found any satisfactory alternative to a chronological order.)

Once again I have separated my dream poems from the rest, because they have to be read in a different way. Despite misgivings about anything incomplete, I agreed with my four selectors in wishing to represent the two longer sequences 'Travelling' and 'In Suffolk' – poems different in kind and structure, as well as in length, from my other work. Though the sequences as a whole are held together by repetition and development, they could neither be omitted here nor printed in full, as they were in the books *Variations* and *Collected Poems*. If our extracts from them are more puzzling than the complete texts, new readers, if any, are referred to those books.

M.H.

Hölderlin

Tübingen, December 1842

Diotima is dead, and silent
The island's singing bird.
The temple I raised from ruin
Fallen again.

Where is the flame I stoked from ashes
Of the mind? Where are the heroes
And my pulsing song?
Nothing stirs on the lakes of time.
Give back my agony,
O stir the forest's sap,
Sweep my slow blood.

And yet, no caged old panther I,
Pacing my madness. These muttered words
Are gates, not bars, where only I can pass.
This is my wisdom, where no flowers grow,
No weeds, this is my peace.

I am calm now, with the world
Locked out, bowed to the door;
My meadow end is pensioned by the gods.
They did not hear,
O crippled Fate, the grimy idol's
Golden teeth led them away.

I have no tears to mourn forsaken gods
Or my lost voice.
This is my wisdom where no laughter sounds,
No sighs, this is my peace.

Glory is gone, and the swimming clouds;
My dumb hand grips the frozen sky,
A black bare tree in the winter dusk.

Sentry Duty

His box is like a coffin, but erect.
The night is dull as death. He must not sleep,
But leans against the boards. The night winds creep
Around his face, while the far stars reflect
The awful emptiness of heart and brain,
And trembling wires intone a requiem.
(If they were Sirens he would follow them
Anywhere, anywhere, to their lush domain.)

But no one passes. A stray cat cries out,
The moon emerges from a cloud's dark rim,
And vanishes. He walks, and turns about.

Next day no sad unrest bewilders him
Who'd seen the planets fall into a trance,
The earth shed lustre and significance.

Rimbaud in Africa

As tradesmen say everything is worth what it will fetch, so probably every mental pursuit takes its reality and worth from the ardour of the pursuer, being in itself a Nothing. JOHN KEATS

1

Poems? You would like me to write more poems?
About dusk in the desert, perhaps, dates, camels and thirst?
Mirages?
        Why not, if you pay me well.

So they're talking of me in the salons.
I know the sequence: the salons after the littérateurs,
And lastly the dons.
Verlaine has written about me, called me a poète maudit?
Do they have to put even the curse on paper,
Isn't even the curse my own?

You ask me to think of glory:
An adolescent's dream. I am growing up.
Yes, I hear old Paul has been taught
To sigh most endearingly:
Ladies are weeping over 'Sagesse'.
I leave the glory to him.

So they're talking of me in the salons.
Let them talk! Their words cannot reach me now.
I've travelled far to earn an honest living.

2

Any strumming will do, if it titillates.
There's your glory for which a poet pawns his soul
And vivisects himself –
A topic for the bored, a thesis for the dons.
For that we torment ourselves,
Practise exquisite contortions, melodious anguish.
The birds make happier music.

11

Often at evening a fair pervades
A village with music of roundabouts.
Yet windows are not shut,
And old men's faces melt
With memories. The tunes are flat,
Neat and mechanic as the lives they led.
But if a poet were to raise his voice
Above the noise of traffic
And for a moment silence
Laughter and bargaining and scolding,
The cries of little children would not cease,
Nor a cow raise her head from the grass.
Only, in the asylum garden
One inmate would stop his ears,
And another smile.

3

I was clever when I was young –
Good at Latin, better at blasphemy.
I built myself a hell and furnished it,
Disdained the comfort of other people's heaven.
My hysteria was cosmogenetic, but did not change
One grain of sand in the real world.
A little experience has made me dull.

I have travelled far,
But all my journeys are like the scenes of a play,
Shifting but half-real only;
For I know the players, who are
Always the same, everywhere,
And I know something of the playwright too.

London, Cairo, Paris, Addis-Abbaba
Or villages of the Ardennes:
This earth was made for tourists.
But ask a soldier how he liked the pyramids,
And he'll say that beer is bad in Egypt
And expensive too,
While in Turkey vodka is cheap,

Though the girls are plain.
The Sphinx, at best, makes him regret
The Arc de Triomphe or the Nelson Column.
My journeys are like a soldier's,
Passionless.

Tell my friends in Paris, therefore,
That Rimbaud is dead and likes it,
That even if he were to return
They would not know him, nor he them.
If they speak of a boy
Who wrote verses and thought the angels dumb,
Tell them that thirst is never comic
And that the drunken boat is sober now,
Leaking and battered, only just afloat.
Tell them I do not care
Whether they praise or damn it when it sinks.

Paddington Canal

A mocking mirror, the black water turns
Tall houses upside down, makes learned men
Walk on their heads in squares of burning light;
Lovers like folded bats hang in a kiss,
Swaying as if a breeze could sever them.
The barges, giant sea-birds fast asleep,
Lie on the surface, moored and motionless;
Then, drowning gently, are drawn down to join
The sunken lovers and the acrobats.

Out of the grim dimensions of a street
Slowly I see another landscape grow
Downwards into a lost reality;
A magic mirror, the black water tells
Of a reversed Atlantis wisely built
To catch and to transform
The wasted substance of our daily acts,
Accommodate our mad and lovely doubles
In a more graceful city timelessly.

A Poet's Progress

Like snooker balls thrown on the table's faded green,
Rare ivory and weighted with his best ambitions,
At first his words are launched: not certain what they mean,
He loves to see them roll, rebound, assume positions
Which – since not he – some power beyond him has assigned.
But now the game begins: dead players, living critics
Are watching him – and suddenly one eye goes blind,
The hand that holds the cue shakes like a paralytic's,
Till every thudding, every clinking sound portends
New failure, new defeat. Amazed, he finds that still
It is not he who guides his missiles to their ends
But an unkind geometry that mocks his will.

If he persists, for years he'll practise patiently,
Lock all the doors, learn all the tricks, keep noises out,
Though he may pick a ghost or two for company
Or pierce the room's inhuman silence with a shout.
More often silence wins; then soon the green felt seems
An evil playground, lawless, lost to time, forsaken,
And he a fool caught in the water weeds of dreams
Whom only death or frantic effort can awaken.

At last, a master player, he can face applause,
Looks for a fit opponent, former friends, emerges;
But no one knows him now. He questions his own cause,
And has forgotten why he yielded to those urges,
Took up a wooden cue to strike a coloured ball.
Wise now, he goes on playing; both his house and heart
Unguarded solitudes, hospitable to all
Who can endure the cold intensity of art.

The Dual Site

To my twin who lives in a cruel country
    I wrote a letter at last;
For my bones creaked out in our long silence
    That seven years had passed,

Seven whole years since he and I
    By word or token exchanged
The message I dare not do without:
    That still we are not estranged,

Though I watch figures in a city office
    And he the waves of the sea,
Keeping no count since he hardly cares
    What happens to him or to me;

Since to names and numbers he closed his head
    When, children still, we were parted,
Chose birth and death for his calendar,
    But leaves the dates uncharted,

Being one who forgets what I remember,
    Who knows what I do not,
Who has learnt the ways of otter and raven
    While I've grown polyglot.

Lately I found a cactus in flower
    And feared for his apple-trees,
Dozed in the club and saw his cattle
    Drag with a foul disease,

And my bones grown stiff with leaning and lying
    Cried out that I'll labour in vain
Till I help my twin to rebuild his hovel
    That's open to wind and rain.

So I sent him a note, expecting no answer,
    And a cheque he'd never cash,
For I knew he was one who'd smile if he heard
    His own roof come down with a crash,

But above the porpoise-leaping bay
  Where ploughshare fin and tail
Cut furrows the foam-flecked sea fills up
  He'd stand in the swishing gale,

Calm as the jackdaws that nest in crannies
  And no more prone to doubt,
With gull and cormorant perched on the rocks
  Would wait the weather out.

Yet he wrote by return: "Have no fear for your dwelling
  Though dry-rot gnaws at the floors;
Only lighten their load of marble and metal,
  Keep clear the corridors,

Move out the clocks that clutter your study,
  And the years will leave you alone:
Every frame I know of lasts long enough,
  Though but cardboard, wood or bone.

And spare me your nightmares, brother, I beg you,
  They make my daemons laugh,
They scare the spirits that rarely will visit
  A man with no wand or staff,

With no symbol, no book and no formula,
  No lore to aid him at all,
Who wherever he walks must find the image
  That holds his mentors in thrall.

But your waking cares put down on paper
  For me to give to the wind,
That the seed may fall and the dry leaf crumble,
  Not a wisp he left behind

Of the tangle that hides the dual site
  Where even you and I
Still may meet again and together build
  One house before we die."

A Child Accepts

"Later", his mother said; and still those little hands
Clawed air to clutch the object of their need,
Abandoned as birds to winds or fishes to tide,
Pure time that is timeless, time untenanted.

"Later", she said; and the word was cold with death,
Opposing space to his time, intersecting his will.
He summoned the cry of a wounded animal,
Mindless Adam whose world lies crushed by the Fall,

But suddenly mended his face and far from tears
Grew radiant, relaxed, letting his hands drop down.
"Later", he sang, and was human, fallen again,
Received into mind, his dubious, his true demesne.

"Later", he played with the word, and later will envy
The freedom of birds and fishes for ever lost,
When, migrant in mind whom wind and water resist,
Here he must winter in body, bound to the coast;

Or, not all his "laters" past, perhaps he'll know
That the last releases: reversed, his needs will throng
Homeward to nest in his head and breed among
Those hidden rocks that wrecked him into song.

Under the Lime-tree...
(From the Middle High German of Walther von der Vogelweide)

Under the lime-tree,
By the heath,
Where with my well-beloved I lay,
You can go and see –
Pleasant both –
Flowers and grass we broke that day.
Where the forest meets the dale:
Tandaradee!
 Sweetly sang the nightingale.

Here we were meeting;
But already
My well-beloved was waiting there.
Such was his greeting,
Gracious Lady,
That ever since I've walked on air.
Did he kiss me? Yes, and well:
Tandaradee!
 Look how red my lips are still.

With the wild flowers
There my love
Made a lavish bed for me;
This bed of ours,
Should you pass above,
Will make you laugh most heartily.
By the roses you can trace –
Tandaradee!
 Where my head lay in that place.

Had anyone seen us
Lying there,
(God grant none did!) I'd be ashamed.
What passed between us
Is our affair,
Never to be known or named
But by us and one small bird –
Tandaradee!
 Which may never breathe a word.

19

Spring Song in Winter

Too long, too long
I gathered icicles in spring
To thread them for a melting song;
And in midsummer saw the foliage fall,
Too foolish then to sing
How leaf and petal cling
Though wind would bear them to the root of all.

Now winter's come, and winter proves me wrong:
Dark in my garden the dead,
Great naked briars, have spread,
So vastly multiplied
They almost hide
The single shrub to share whose blossoming
Blood on cold thorns my fingers shed.

Homage to the Weather

A tide, high tide of golden air.

Where, till this moment, were the bees?
And when no hum made for the honeysuckle,
Fumbled,
Became a body,
Clung and drank,
Spindrift, disowned, the petals hung,
And wait, let go was what the summer meant.

A corner of the garden, ivy on broken slats,
A branch with orange puffs: buddleia globosa.
Between two gusts a flood of golden air,
Mere hush, perhaps, abeyance – but the bees
Clinging and drinking.

Walls they brought with them: black courtyard in Paris,
A bit of marble, tumbled, dust on leaves,
A goldfish pond, the traffic not remote,
Audible, yet excluded;
Flowering tree or shrub in any weathered city,
Walls to contain a quietness, a quiver,
Fulfilment of the year, bees to be stilled.

Between two gusts, cold waves, the golden tide.

Tides

To wake without fail when milk bottles shake in their racks,
Scrape one's face in the morning, every morning,
Take the same route to work and say 'good morning'
To the same row of scraped or powdered faces –
I cursed the roundness of this earth, I raged
At every self-perpetuating motion,
Hated the sea, that basher of dumb rock,
For all her factory of weeds and fishes,
The thumps, the thuds, the great reverberations –
Too much in rhythm; jarring, but by rote.

The metronome it was in my own head
That ticked and ticked; caged cricket in my head
That chirped and chirped until I had no ear
For syncopation, counterpoint of stillness
Beating against all music – of the sea,
Of birds and men, of season and machine,
Even of cricket and of metronome.
In silence I learned to listen; in the dark to look.

And unrepeatable now each morning's light
Modulates, shuffles, probes the daily faces
Often too suddenly different, like the street,
This weathered wall re-pointed, that new one cracked,
Apple trees that I prune while I forget
The shape of last year's boughs, cankered or grown,
And where that stump is, one that died in blossom;
Forget the hill's curve under the aerial masts.

No, wheels, grind on; seasons, repeat yourselves,
Milk bottles, rattle; familiars, gabble 'good morning';
Breed, hatch, digest your weeds and fishes, sea,
Omit no beat, nor rise to tidal waves.
Various enough the silences cut in
Between the rock cave's boom and the small wader's cry.

A Horse's Eye

I did not stop today at the five-barred gate,
Did not wait for the old white draught-horse at grass,
Unshod, unharnessed these many years; walked past,
Preoccupied, but something made me look back:
Her head was over the gate, her neck was straight,
But I caught her eye, a wicked, reproachful look
From one small eye slanted in my direction.
What right, I defied the old mare, what right had she
To expect caresses, the grass foolishly plucked
For her hanging lip, her yellow, broken teeth
And her great historical belly? Of course she's a relic,
Curious now as the old white country house
That stood empty and alluring in the wood behind her
Till converted into flats – not as useless as she,
Who will never become a tractor! What farmer would care?
Only some town-bred, animist, anthropomorphic rambler
Or week-end motorist looking for what he's lost.

I walked on; but plainly her glance had spoken to me,
As an old peasant's might in a foreign country,
Communicating neither words nor thought, but the knowledge
Of flesh that has suffered labour in rain and wind,
Fed, relaxed, enjoyed and opposed every season.
Broken now. Close to death. And how differently broken
From that Cossack mare the clumsiest rider could sit,
All speed and nerve and power that somehow responded
To the faintest twitch of a will less tense than her own!
Wild nature still; her eye no peasant's eye,
But lava under glass, tellurian fire contained.

As for the old white mare, her reproach was just:
Because she was too intelligible I had passed her by,
Because not alien enough, but broken as men are broken,
Because the old white house was converted now,
The wood about to be felled, a tractor chugging
Beyond the hill, and awkwardly she trotted
On legs too thin for her belly bloated with age,
Alone in her meadow, at grass, and close to death.

Blind Man

He can hear the owl's flight in daylight
When, surprised, on silky wings it shoots
From a low perch; and by the open window at night
The stag-beetles blundering in the hedges
On the far side of the meadow. Geese half a mile away
Honk near as hooters of swerving cars
And do not alarm him. Indifferently he awaits
Dogs that he feared when they slunk or bounded
Visible at him, as if in his carapace
Of darkness for ever secure from harm,
Wombed and housed and coffined within a wound
That has hardened to armour. The screech and the hum
Blend and subside in a resonant quiet,
Shapes he has fumbled to feel fall back
Into unbroken space when his hands forget them,
And still are present in his no man's land;
Above the nightmare tamed by light's extinction
The apple that hangs unplucked, grown fabulous.

Conformist

Branded in childhood, for thirty years he strove
To hide the scar, and truly to believe
In the true fundaments of that commonweal
Which once had outlawed him beyond repeal,
And with true awe, true gratitude, true love
Would gaze upon the incorruptible guard
Before the gate – the keeper of his peace
Who in mean streets could live anonymous...

Until conformity brought its reward:
A crested, gilt-edged card. The great gate opened,
A pair of stiff lips cracked and let him pass
Into those halls his half-life's dreams had deepened;
And out again... to breathe the ownerless air
Night sky transfigured, lucent, fresh and clear
After the ceilings puffed in emulation.
His own place found at last; his own self found –
Outside, outside – his heritage regained
By grace of exile, of expropriation.

What had he seen, ushered behind the gate?
The dress and furniture of his own terrors,
A glittering medal pinned on his own wound,
And, at the heart, an empty hall of mirrors.

Healed now, of health, unmasked, of honesty,
In, out again he passed, with one smile met
The questioning eyes of flunkey, potentate,
Townsman and guard shrunk to complicity,
All one to him at one with every station
Since none was his, nor ever now could be;
Come late into the freedom his from birth,
To breathe the air, and walk the ownerless earth.

The Moment

Trapped in the whorls of a conch time roared.
Eye, mind met walls,
Could neither enter nor rebound,
The moment lost in plotting for the act.

Sleep cracked the shell,
In lidded eyes unlocked the cells of light,
Undid no knot long fingered,
Traced no new shape, nor any sign but this:

Morning, the slanted beams
Through low dark boughs and the bunched leaves of bushes.
A streak of lawn illumined? Yet
It was not grass or grain of wood and leaf
That held the moment whole. It was the angle:
Sunlight, and how it fell.

Quince and Blackthorn

Trunk hard and ridged, more fit for hedges
If more than trunk, not by a curious marriage
Disarmed of spikes, lopped and tamed in an orchard
To bear this wealth of delicate boughs cascading,
Flounced pink, downed gold, devoured by parasites
Strange to his grain's potential, fostered disapproving.

Crest lithe and light, the weather's dancer
But for the bitter moods for ever rising
From his dark roots and the dank clay beneath;
Fearing each leaf-fall, fruit-fall, yearly diminished
Not for his sake, to swell the festering humus
That breeds and buries, feeds and chokes unheeding.

Gardener indeed, who grafted quince on blackthorn,
Binding two kinds, two minds, by one sap mellowed,
Lifelong divided, indivisible lifelong in labour
For fruit not like the sun's gold or his aborted berries
Gratuitous, never learned the art of undoing,
From wounded fibre exacts the blossom whole!

Trunk hard and ridged, more fit for hedges
But for this wealth, her delicate boughs cascading
From his dark roots and the dank clay beneath;
By dint of wealth, downed gold by one sap mellowed,
Grown more than trunk or his aborted berries:
Crest lithe and light, the weather's dancer.

Security

1

So he's got there at last, been received as a partner –
In a firm going bankrupt;
Found the right place (walled garden), arranged for a mortgage –
But they're pulling the house down
To make room for traffic.

Worse winds are rising. He takes out new policies
For his furniture, for his life,
At a higher premium
Against more limited risks.

2

Who can face the winds, till the panes crack in their frames?
And if a man faced them, what in the end could he do
But look for shelter like all the rest?
The winds too are afraid, and blow from fear.

3

I hear my children at play
And recall that one branch of the elm-tree looks dead;
Also that twenty years ago now I could have been parchment
Cured and stretched for a lampshade,
Who now have children, a lampshade
And the fear of those winds.

I saw off the elm-tree branch
To find that the wood was sound;
Mend the fences yet again,
Knowing they'll keep out no one,
Let alone the winds.
For still my children play
And shall tomorrow, if the weather holds.

Errors

A short-wave station gabbles and hums –
The newly filled tea-pot.
Turtle doves coo in the corner –
Something vibrates as I type.
Outside, a mechanical saw –
Guinea fowl screeching.
A pheasant's repeated hoot –
Cars on the new road.
I bend and smell tom-cats –
Blackcurrant bushes;
Mimosa –
Meadowsweet.

I appoint my two eyes judge,
Sole upholders now of the decencies
Of reason, identity, place,
Yet from Thames to Riviera
Am wholly transported:
Meadowsweet to mimosa,
The blue-white-silver, yellow-tufted trees
On the mountainside
Long unvisited, never missed.
And the daily hill gone.

Oxford

Years on the Gothic rack:
Bells crashing down on green water,
Lashing the tree trunks for growing,
The meadows for lying flat.

And the flushed girls laughing
At calf love.
Planting banderillas
That itched and dropped, but to burn –
All moved on, moved on

Not where the arches would fling them,
Not to a cloistered garden
Nor yet to the riverside,
The willows, the weeping willows,

To pins and needles in armchairs,
Shrilling of telephone, doorbell,
A well-mannered print or two
Of towers, Gothic, black
Against trim foliage, blue sky.

At Fifty-Five

Country dances
Bird calls
The breathing of leaves after thunder –
And now fugues.
Modulations "impolite"
Syncopations "unnatural".
No more clapping of hands
When moonshine had opened their tear-ducts
Or fanfares clenched
Heroic nerves –
But a shaking of heads:
Can't help it, our decomposer,
Can't hear his own blundering discords.

As if one needed ears
For anything but chit-chat about the weather,
Exchange of solicitude, malice –
And birdsong, true, the grosser, the bouncing rhythms.
Uncommunicative? Yes. Unable
'Like beginners to learn from nightingales'.
Unwilling, too, for that matter –
To perform, to rehearse, to repeat,
To take in, to give back.

In time out of time, in the concert no longer concerted.
But the music all there, what music,
Where from –
Water that wells from gravel washed clean by water.
All there – inaudible thrushes
Outsinging the nightingales, peasants
Dancing weightless, without their shoes –
Where from, by what virtue? None.
By what grace but still being here, growing older?
The water cleansed by gravel washed clean by water.

Fugue, ever itself –
And ever growing,

Gathering up – itself,
Plunging – into itself,
Rising – out of itself,
Fathoming – only itself
To end, not to end its flowing –
No longer itself –
In a stillness that never was.

For a Family Album

Four heads in one lamp's light
And each head bowed into peculiar darkness,
Reading, drawing, alone.
A camera would have caught them, held them there
Half-lit in the room's warm halflight,
Left them, refused to tell
How long till that lamp was broken,
Your hair pinned up or cut or tinted or waved.

I cannot even describe them, caught no more
Than a flash of light that ripped open
The walls of our half-lit room;
Or the negative – a black wedge
Rammed into light so white that it hurt to look.

Leave this page blank.
You'd neither like nor believe
The picture no lens could have taken:

Tied to my rooted bones
In your chairs you were flying, flying.

In a Cold Season

I

Words cannot reach him in his prison of words
Whose words killed men because those men were words
Women and children who to him were numbers
And still are numbers though reiterated
Launched into air to circle out of hearing
And drop unseen, their metal shells not broken.
Words cannot reach him though I spend more words
On words reporting words reiterated
When in his cage of words he answered words
That told how with his words he murdered men
Women and children who were words and numbers
And he remembered or could not remember
The words and numbers they reiterated
To trap in words the man who killed with words.
Words cannot reach the children, women, men
Who were not words or numbers till they died
Because ice-packed in terror shrunk minds clung
To numbers words that did not sob or whimper
As children do when packed in trucks to die
That did not die two deaths as mothers do
Who see their children packed in trucks to die.

II

Yet, Muse of the IN-trays, OUT-trays,
Shall he be left uncelebrated
For lack of resonant numbers calculated
To denote your hero, and our abstract age?
Rather in the appropriate vocabulary
Let a memorandum now be drawn up –
Carbon copies to all whom it may concern –
A monument in kind, a testimonial
To be filed for further reference
And to circulate as required.
Adolf Eichmann, civil servant (retired):
A mild man, meticulous in his ways,

34

As distinctly averse to violence
As to all other irregularities
Perpetrated in his presence,
Rudeness of speech or deportment,
Infringements of etiquette
Or downright incompetence, the gravest offence;
With a head for figures, a stable family life,
No abnormalities.

Never lost his temper on duty
Even with subordinates, even with elements earmarked
For liquidation;
Never once guilty of exceeding his authority
But careful always to confine his ambitions
Within the limits laid down for personnel of his grade.
Never, of course, a maker of policy,
But in its implementation at office level,
Down to the detailed directive, completely reliable;
Never, perhaps, indispensable,
Yet difficult to replace
Once he had mastered the formalities
Of his particular department
And familiarized himself with his responsibilities
As a specialist in the organization
Of the transport and disposal of human material –
In short, an exemplary career.

III

Words words his words – and half his truth perhaps
If blinking, numb in moonlight and astray
A man can map the landmarks trace the shapes
That may be mountains icebergs or his tears
And he whose only zeal was to convert
Real women children men to words and numbers
Added to be subtracted leaving nothing
But aggregates and multiples of nothing
Can know what made him adept in not knowing
Feel what it was he could not would not feel –
And caged in words between their death his death

35

No place no time for memory to unfreeze
The single face that would belie his words
The single cry that proved his numbers wrong.

Probing his words with their words my words fail.
Cold cold with words I cannot break the shell
And almost dare not lest his whole truth be
To have no core but unreality.

IV

I heard no cry, nor saw her dying face,
Have never known the place, the day,
Whether by bullet, gas or deprivation
They finished her off who was old and ill enough
To die before long in her own good time;
Only that when they came to march her out of her human world,
Creaking leather couch, mementoes, widow's urn,
They made her write a postcard to her son in England.
'Am going on a journey'; and that all those years
She had refused to travel even to save her life.
Too little I know of her life, her death,
Forget my last visit to her at the age of nine,
The goodbye like any other that was the last,
Only recall that she, mother of five, grandmother,
Freely could share with a child all her little realm;
Recall her lapdog who trembled and snapped up cheese –
Did they kill her lapdog also, or drive him away? –
And the bigger dog before that, a French bulldog, stuffed
To keep her company still after his early death.
Three goldfishes I recall, one with a hump on his back
That lived for years though daily she brushed her fishes
Under the kitchen tap to keep them healthy and clean;
And how she conspired with us children,
Bribed us with sweets if we promised not to tell
Our father that she, who was diabetic,
Kept a pillbox of sweets in her handbag
To eat like a child in secret –
When neither could guess that sweets would not cause her death.
A wireless set with earphones was part of the magic

She commanded and freely dispensed,
Being childlike herself and guileless and wise...

Too little I know of her wisdom, her life,
Only that, guileless, she died deprived
Of her lapdog even, stuffed bulldog and pillbox of sweets.

V

And yet and yet I would not have him die
Caged in his words their words – one deadly word
Setting the seal on unreality
Adding one number to the millions dead
Subtracting nothing from death dividing nothing
Silencing him who murdered words with words
Not one shell broken, not one word made flesh.
Nor in my hatred would imprison him
Who never free in fear and hatred served
Another's hatred which again was fear
So little life in him he dared not pity
Or if he pitied dared not act on pity;
But show him pity now for pity's sake
And for their sake who died for lack of pity;
Break from the husk at last one naked grain
That still may grow where the massed carrion lay
Bones piled on bones their only mourners bones
The inconceivable aggregate of the dead
Beyond all power to mourn or to avenge;
See man in him spare woman child in him
Though in the end he neither saw nor spared –
Peel off the husk for once and heed the grain,
Plant it though he sowed nothing poisoned growth;
Dare break one word and words may yet be whole.

Treblinka

That winter night they were burning corpses
And from the bonfire, flooding the whole camp
Flared purple and blue and red and orange and gold,
The many colours of Joseph's coat, who was chosen.
Not cold for once we at the barrack windows
Blinked and listened; the opera singer,
Unafraid for once, found his full voice and gave it
To words, to a music that gushed like blood from a wound:
Eli, Eli...his question too in whose name
Long we'd been dirt to be wiped off, dust to be dispersed –
Older than he, old as the silence of God.
In that light we knew it; and the complaint was praise,
Was thankfulness for death, the lost and the promised land,
The gathering up at last, all our hundred hues
Fierce in one radiance gathered by greater darkness,
The darkness that took our kings, David and Solomon
Who living had burnt with the same fire;
All our hundred languages gathered again in one silence.

To live was the law; though to live – and not only here –
Was a hundred times over to spit in our own faces,
Wipe ourselves out of creation, scatter as dust,
Eat grass, and the dung that feeds grass.
The grass, the dung, the spittle – here we saw them consumed,
Even these bodies fit in the end to yield light.

Back in a room in a house in a street in a town
I forget the figures, remember little but this:
That to live is not good enough: everything, anything
Proved good enough for life – there, and not only there.
Yet we lived, a few of us, perhaps with no need but this:
To tell of the fire in the night and briefly to flare like the dead.

The House Martins I

Pines I remember, the air crisp.
Here, in a haze, elms I see,
Do not see, and hills hiding the river.

But the roof is generous,
Can preserve nests. And again the martins mutter
Their small-talk, daily domestic twitter
After those miles, deadly to some,
Over glaciers, over high waves.

Arrived, arrived in whatever wind,
To ride all winds and, housed on the windy side,
Warm with their own blood the cold mud walls.

The House Martins II

1

Fifteen years later. From under an older roof.
In weather blown in from the north,
With roses that rot in bud, sodden.
In a colder, windier county:
Again that muttering, on the windy side of the house.

Fluttering exits, a jerkier tacking
Than the swallows' that, flashier, shoot
Into flight from their perches indoors,
On the sheltered side,
Through a square gap in the panes
Less wide than their wingspan.
Or the swallows' homing, a headlong dive
Into familiar darkness.

Never loud as the swifts that shriek as they swoop and glide
High up in great circles, and mate on the wing.

Again that muttering. A muted gabble,
Low gurgle under the eaves.

The smallest words are not small enough
To record them, the martins, and their small recurrence,
Their small defiance, of more and more.

So I repeat: fifteen years later.
Here they are. Again. Still.
And can perpetrate no infinities, for comfort,
Nor mouth the metaphors that will damn my kind
The summer I see their empty nests.

The Jackdaws

Gone, I thought, had not heard them for years;
Gone like the nuthatch, the flycatcher,
Like the partridges from the bulldozed hill.
Now it was I who was going,
And they were back, or had never gone,
Chucking, bickering up on the elm's bare branches.

I forgot the changes, the chores,
Jackdaw's corpse in the water tank,
Jackdaw's nest, jackdaw's dry bones, dry feathers
Stuffed down the chimneys –
No longer mine to clear.
I heard them, I saw them again in the cold clean air
And, going, my tenure ended,
Brought in the harvest of three thousand weathers,
The soot, the silver, the hubbub on trees left behind.

Removed

Lost, the land looks away,
The light in the orchard glassy
Like the eyes of our white cat
Who before the vans came
Lay down there and died,
Leaving the last of her many litters
Unweaned in a bramble thicket,
Hair on end, hissing.
And she whom I buried there
Prowls through the high grass.

She belongs to the elm's black bulk,
Silvery green of the apple trees
And the faint wind that carries
The lowing of heifers up
From the farm she was born in;
Whose meadows are raw soil, churned,
Milking-shed, barn disused,
Gate hinges broken;
To the hills beyond it, their beeches
Huddled and bunched, a thick cloud.

Wholly now, in late halflight,
The land disowns us.
From branches a century old
For the first, for the last time
Overripe pears drop.
And tail in the air, sniffing,
Ears pricked, deaf to my call,
Out of an empty house
Into the hedgehog's, the owl's garden
Walks a white cat.

Home

1

Red house on the hill.
Windward, the martins' mud nests
Year after year filled
With a twittering, muttering brood.
On the still side, hedged,
Apples turned in on themselves
A damp, dull summer long
Until ripe. Rare hum of bees.
The two great elms where the jackdaws roosted,
Beyond them the wild half-acre
With elm scrub rising, rambling
From old roots –
Never tamed or possessed
Though I sawed, scythed, dug
And planted saplings, walnut,
Hazel, sweet chestnut,
A posthumous grove.
And the meadow's high grass,
Flutter of day-moth over
Mallow, cranesbill, vetch:
All razed, bole and brick,
Live bough and empty nest,
Battered, wrenched, scooped
Away to be dumped, scrapped.

2

A place in the mind, one place in one or two minds
Till they move on, confused, cluttered with furniture, landmarks.
The house let me go in the end, sprung no more leaks or cracks,
The garden ceased to disown me with bindweed, ground elder.

What's left is whole: a sketch or two, a few photographs,
A name on old maps. And the weather. The light.

43

3

Seeing martins fly
Over a tiled roof, not mine,
Over concrete, tarmac,
A day-moth cling
To a nettle flower,
Hearing children, not mine,
Call out in a laurel-hedged orchard,
I'm there again. Home.

Shakespeare Road, S.E. 24

Not marble. Yet low down
Under the windows of this corner shop
A multicoloured frieze,
Crazy patchwork of little bits,
Hand-made, one man's defiance.
No picture postcards and no statuettes;
No call for them here
As in that other place
Where now they look for him,
His absence is bought and sold,

Grassily quiet now
In orchards walled or hedged
Sweeten mutations of his leathercoat,
Pomewater, costard, codling, applejohn,
Russetting too, the rare, the dying savours.
Blackbird and thrush and linnet, the same, the same,
Sing to no ear quite open,
No eye quite open dares nor lens can follow
Business the winds and clouds transact
With light, green light, half-sunbeams with the leaves.

Here, then. Look for him here
Where boys ride bicycles over rubble, skirting
A grey van gutted of its engine, dumped
Outside the Council Works;
Down a long row
Of dingy terrace houses
And, facing it, a barred and spiked embankment
Of willow herb and refuse, depots and railways sidings,
His road, and anyone's,
With relics of a sort,
The rag and bone man's horse,
The rag and bone man's wares,
Perhaps his book, patched and passed on,
Lived in, moved through.

S-Bahn
Berlin, 1965

The gunpowder smell,
The corpses have been disposed of,
The gas rose up, diffused.
Kaiser, President, Führer
Have come and gone,
The housewives in funny hats
Came from the suburbs to shop,
Came from the central flats
To litter the woods and lakes,
Gushing about 'Natur'.
What remains is the carriage smell,
Tobacco smoke and heaters in stale air,
Indefinable, changeless
Monkey-house odour
Heavy on seats as hard
But emptier,
Now that the train connects
One desolation with another,
Punctual as ever, moves through the rubble
Of Kaiser, President, Führer,
Is halted, searched and cleared
Of those it would serve too well
This winter when, signalled on, it crosses
The frontier, no man's land,
Carrying only the smell
Over to neon lights
Past the deeper snow
Around dead financiers' villas
And the pine-woods' darkness
Into the terminus
Where one foreigner stamps cold feet.

Teesdale

Walked up to the scar.
Walked down to the beck.
Walked on wet hay, on heather,
On limestone, on spongy grass,
Learning the shapes of tiniest lichen and rock plant,
Marsh crowfoot and meadow campanula,
The various yellows and reds of the monkey flower,
Habitat of juniper, of mountain ash,
Haunts of curlew and grouse,
The wide distribution of starlings.

Bathed in clear shallows, in pools,
In deeper, peat-coloured water.
Saw dawn and dusk, noonlight, moonlight, starlight –
Caught a snatch or two of the small-talk of place.

When the wind began to sing,
Articulate, with human voices from nowhere,
There was an end to small-talk,
Not one peewit to be heard.

When the mist came down
There was no pasture, no copse,
Only the smell of hay getting lost in moorland,
The green and the crimson moss drowning.

Wind and mist –
They took all the rest away.

Loach

Loach, slimy loam, embodied, shaped,
Articulate in him. The strength, the softness.
His delicate eye draws light to riverbeds,
Through water draws our weather.

In gravel, mud, he lurks,
Gravel-coloured for safety,
Streamlined only to shoot
Back into mud or merge
In gravel, motionless, lurking.

Low he forages, late,
His radar whiskers alive
To a burrowing worm's commotion,
Tomorrow's thunder;
Advances bounding, prods
And worries a quiet pasture,
Munches athwart, in a cloud.

More than loam, at times he must rise,
His need, his weakness, richly to breathe;
Will rest on weeds, inconspicuous,
But, worse, gulp air, blow bubbles aft,
Expose a belly naked and pale, transparent.
Stickleback, minnow
Gape at his wriggling, uncertain
Whether to nibble or flee.

Perch can swallow him whole.

In Massachusetts I
For G.E.

1

Crows yap in the wood. This murmur
Is chipmunks, they dive
When dead branches crunch underfoot.

I cross fields of maize,
Papery now in the wind,
Make for the farther woods –

The maple's reds and the maple's yellows
Are flames above, in the sun,
Are embers below me –

And come to a track, a clearing:
Mortuary of metal,
Motor cars dumped, a blue,
A chrome and white holding out
Against the fire of the years.
How long, till rust takes them back?

Or this homestead, flimsy, a bungalow.
This farmer scything
The purple black-berried weed
Doesn't know its name. Poison,
He says, a Pole, unfamiliar still
With all but the sandy soil
And the ways of his cattle, deep
In stalks of goldenrod, of michaelmas daisies;
Doesn't know his collie's breed:
So foreign, he hardly looks up.

No need for words. But this chirping,
What body, cricket or frog
Hides in the pines, what feathers,

Russet or crimson, ruffle
Over that little cry,
See me, see me, the more to be here?

On. A brook winds
Through the wood. Against black leaves
Russet markings on crayfish tails
Remind me. (Forward they crawled, feeling their way,
Backward they shot, blindly.)

Banks and logs I search,
For turtles –
Too late in the year.

But motionless there a beaked fish
Shines, his knife-blade flank mottled and opal-green –
Never known, never seen before.

And now, at the pond-side, my looking
Is referred to the sky,
To tree-trunks, any tree-trunks, and ubiquitous water.

Back to the meadows, then,
Silk exploding from milkweed, little rootstock, grain
Soon to be covered by snow, till I am gone,

So that merely to walk under the low sun
I am free, and pass, leaving the signs unread,
These buds too cryptic for my decoding.

On, on, to forget, unlearn it all,
Even the bluejay's name, recalled by no blue wings
Unless they flash once more in those empty spaces
Left by unlearning, by forgetfulness,
Larger each day, as I make for a dark house.

In Massachusetts II

1

In a dark house too
There is movement, a coming and going.
The bluejay's cry
Rises above the noise of a street
Where the cars are double-parked:
Blue wings, olive, grey and off-white
Of the underside not recalled
But seen, grown familiar as all
The coming and going, all
Who came and went.
To the door of a dark house
The postman brings
Words that will not be read.
Still
This yapping is crows, whether
I listen or
Am half-deaf with the buzzing,
The rattling, humming, shrilling
That turn on, turn off
By day and by night in
A house that's not mine;
Whether I write for a living
Friend or one dead.

2

And of nothing now that concerns
Him or me. Of the black pond
And quivering light, yellow
Of leaves reflected, yellow
Of leaves drifting down
To float for a while;
Of sunbeams, turning.
Of the snake,
Blackish and yellow-striped,
On the bank, head raised

51

From the coiled length of a body
That pulses, at rest.

There I stand, looking;
And make for no place but
For this, where
We've no business, none.
And the house, bright
Or dark,
Is not ours.

Cat

Unfussy lodger, she knows what she wants and gets it:
Food, cushions, fires, the run of the garden.
I, her night porter in the small hours,
Don't bother to grumble, grimly let her in.
To that coldness she purrs assent,
Eats her fill and outwits me,
Plays hide and seek in the dark house.

Only at times, by chance meeting the gaze
Of her amber eyes that can rest on me
As on a beech-bole, on bracken or meadow-grass,
I'm moved to celebrate the years between us,
The farness and the nearness:
My fingers graze her head.
To that fondness she purrs assent.

Cat, Ageing

Her years measure mine.
So finely set in her ways,
She divines, she sniffs out
Every change in the house,
In the weather, and marks it for me
Though with a flick of an ear
Only, a twitch of her tail.
She foretells convolutions,
Departure, thunderstorm,
By not being there – hiding
Behind the heater. At times
She will play yet, kittenish,
Or hunt; but then gathers
All movement, vanity
Into her great stillness
That contains the whole of herself
And more, of her kind. When she stays there,
Dies, it is me she'll prove mortal.

Cat, Dying

To be silent, sparing of sound,
Was her way; to be still,
Sparing of movement
Save to leap and land
With precision, even when old,
Where she must, on the stove
Or window-sill, on her prey;
Silent, save to express
Satisfaction by purring,
Hunger by gentle mewing,
Care, long ago,
When she called her kittens,
By low tones;
Day after day, for hours on end,
She would share a stillness with me
On my writing table or desk.
Rarely, before she was older than old,
Failing, did a pain draw
Cries from her in a voice not hers
But pain's voice, a howling;
And soon, again and again
She would recompose
Her silence, restored to herself.

Little silence or stillness
Could accrue to her, then,
After the last spasms;
Mouth and eyes wide-open
With the strain of her dying,
With the pain of it:
Cold at last, rigid,
From her sure centre
Hardly she'd shifted.

When, as I buried her
In the quiet marsh, at evening,
The spade struck stone,
It was the harsh noise that jarred,
Not the lean body
Landing, where it must,
Softly, on black soil.

Dowland

"Pleasant are the tears which music weeps"
And durable, black crystal, each drop keeps
When eyes are dry a glimmer of deep light,
But melting, mixed with wine,
Could move the great to offer gold for brine.
Miraculous exchange!
Until that trade grew strange,
Mere dearth of common bread,
True tears, true absence drained the fountainhead,
Put out in utter night
The glimmer, lost to their eyes, lost to mine.
And then I knew what trade
I'd practised unbeknown:
Of blood not ink was my black music made,
Feigned grief to them so sweet because my own
Transmuted nolens volens
By cruel mastery's menial, semper dolens.
But tearless I depart,
Glad that my lute melts no time-serving heart
And deep in crystal glows dark Dowland's art.

The Cello
In Memoriam R.H. 1884-1940

Coffined, draped in black
For years it lay
On top of the white wardrobe
And lying sleepless
In that room
Never I heard
The feathery sonata
Dust must have hummed
On the strings left taut
When his fingers tautened
And became dust,
Deaf and dumb beneath
Black boards, black cloth
Beethoven died in his death.

Many removals have brought me
Closer to where he lay,
Faint music from upstairs
Growing fainter, his house
Drifting away into stillness
And all the voices fading.
Now as I hear
Beethoven re-delivered
By tremulous fingers not his
From another cello's womb
It is dust I breathe,
It is dust that trills:
White feathers whirl
In a black room.

Envoi

Goodbye, words.
I never liked you,
Liking things and places, and
Liking people best when their mouths are shut.

Go out and lose yourselves in a jabbering world,
Be less than nothing, a vacuum
Of which words will beware
Lest by suction, your only assertion, you pull them in.

For that I like you, words.
Self-destroyed, self-dissolved
You grow true.
To what? You tell me, words.

Run, and I'll follow,
Never to catch you up.
Turn back, and I'll run.
So goodbye.

Life and Art II

Because I was writing my poem on sticklebacks –
Day in, day out, again and again
Till I scrapped it, tore up all the drafts –
I forgot to feed them. Mere babies, they gobbled up
Every unarmoured, toothless and spikeless creature
Left alive in the tank,
(Tinier still they'd picked off
The fry of fishes potentially four times their size)
To the last mouthful charged and bit one another
Then weakened and died.

I loved them, of course,
(Nil inhumani etc. – as long as it's nature:
Frogs collide with toads in my creepery garden)
Their fins always aquiver,
Their mottled mackerel sheen,
How they shot, torpedoes in search of ships –
And was full of remorse.
I'd been waiting to see the males
Flush carmine, magnesium blue in the breeding season,
Bravely defend their nests.

Yet my conscience took comfort, too, at the thought:
One love poem less.

Observer

The newspaper in my hands
Reports a four-sided battle
In the streets of a town
I shall never see.
What I see, what I read
Will depend on this war,
The sum and ratio of men
Maimed or killed on each side.

The newspaper in my hands
Omits to count the losses
On a fifth side – the people.
Yet the winner, if any, will count
The people, if any, left over
Because with no people to rule
The winners would not be the winners,
The war itself would not count.

The newspaper in my hands
Will serve to light a fire,
Yesterday's casualties burn
On my grate tomorrow
Or perhaps with dead leaves in the garden;
Tomorrow's newspaper bring me
Headlines that cancel out
Yesterday's interim score.

The newspaper in my hands
Begins to smoulder, to stink
As I read the day's gossip
About business and fashion,
Parties and mergers and
This gossip-monger's views
On a news handout on
A book on a fashion-pimp.

The newspaper in my hands
Begins to rot my hands.
I drop the newspaper, stare:
From my right forefinger
Something obtrudes. I pinch it
And pull out a worm, then another.

I look at my left hand:
Hollowed out, a black stump.
Amid all those woodlice
Scurrying there I spot
A big slug. With a matchstick held
Between worm-eaten fingers
I spear the slug, remove it.
And nothing hurts. Nothing.

Two Photographs

1

At an outdoor table of the Café Heck
In the Munich Hofgarten
Six gentlemen in suits
And stiff white collars
Are sitting over coffee,
Earnestly talking.
The one with a half-moustache
Wears a trilby hat.
The others have hung up theirs,
With their overcoats, on hooks
Clamped to a tree.
The season looks like spring.
The year could be '26.

On a hook otherwise bare
Hangs a dogwhip.

No dog appears in the picture –

An ordinary scene.
Of all the clients
At adjoining tables
None bothers to stare.

2

The year is '33.
The gentleman in a trilby
Is about to board a train.
Behind him stand
Four men in black uniforms.
'For his personal protection'
The Chancellor of the Reich
Carries a dogwhip.

No dog appears in the picture.

The Soul of Man under Capitalism

Looks for its body among
The skyscrapers, tenement blocks
Where a white man's unwise to walk.
At the thought of revolution
Sends kites, balloons into air opaque
With excremental vapours of produce
And sees them vanish, glad
That where they've gone they'll be free.
Meanwhile it feeds refrigerators
With bags of lobster tails, whole sides of prime beef,
Homogenized milk by the gallon; and, hailed by Donuts,
By Steak or Chicken Dinner it glides
Down Main Street emptily, starving
For the smell of newly baked bread.

How to Beat the Bureaucrats
For Reiner Kunze

You can't hit them: they're paper-thin.
You can't hurt them: the paper is not their own.
Yet fight them we must, we who are peaceable
And feel pain, or all will be paper.

They waste your time. It will cost you
More of your time, all the leisure they've left you.
They drain your energy. It will cost you more,
All the wit, all the zest they have left you.

Yes. Fill in those forms. So minutely
That it's harder for them to sift
The relevant facts from those you have sent as a bonus
Than it was for you to compound the mixture.

Invent complications more abstract even than those
They afflict you with. Further sub-divide
Their sub-divisions. Force them to print new forms,
Open departments, engage new specialists

To meet your case. Overfeed their computers,
Till they spew only pure mathematics, deplete themselves
And close down for mystical meditation
On the infinite fractions of nothing. Meanwhile

Bombard the computers' feeders with more and more paper,
Till from paper and ink a man or woman emerges,
Word is made flesh; and, gasping in piles of paper,
They learn again the first of our needs, to breathe.

Ah, and the file will yield up its leaves to unclassified winds,
Inspectors inspect themselves and promptly submit
Applications in triplicate for their own dismissal,
And the clerk will lie down with the client.

Wimbledon on TV: the Ladies' Singles

The commentators clap their traps,
Then like a dripping tap it raps,
Heard from the next room. A brief pause.
More clapping, but of hands: applause.

For whom? For what? I make a guess,
Only to doubt myself, confess:
There's more to it than meets the ear.
Precise it may be, never clear,
Never predictable, this game.
Skill, practice, an athletic frame,
Responses quick, electric, but
Nerves that are steady, don't go phut
When calculation enters in
Because without it few can win,
Yet if they calculate too much
That breaks their rhythm, spoils their touch
So that they hesitate or snatch,
With would-be winners lose the match.
Spontaneous cunning, then? Yes, that:
The tactics of a prowling cat.
And luck. No tactics can forestall
The equivocating net-cord ball,
The little gust of wind that may
Put shots, and players, out of play.

And that's not all; nor tells us why
There's more to it than meets the eye.
Although they call them 'ladies' singles'
Two ladies meet; the meeting mingles
Two chemistries of hope and will
That interact, both mutable.

Add the spectators: mainly British,
Most back Miss W., but, skittish,
They disconcert her, laugh or groan
Just when she needs to feel alone –
The cameras being quite enough

65

To make the easiest round seem tough
To one who senses them. (She does,
And pays for it, begins to fuzz.)
Quixotic, too, they'll switch support
Whenever, poised, she rules the court,
As though appointed by the gods
To punish pride, redress the odds.

Guesswork's no good. I'll go and share
More closely in this weird affair
Which cynics, with a smirk, would bracket
With show-biz – as the tennis racket.
Of course, one wins, the other loses –
But how, is matter for the Muses.
To me, it's drama; tragic, too,
Tense drama, with V.W.
At once protagonist and gauge
Of energies that now will rage,
Now flag. The very way she moves
Transmits the fitful charge, disproves
Glib critics' talk of 'grit' and 'form'.
The needle jumps. She rides a storm,
A storm outside her and inside:
Fate and the Furies will decide
Whether her human gifts avail
Or, too severely surtaxed, fail.

Today they do fail – only just.
I can switch off. Indeed I must,
Thoroughly purged with pity, terror
By each successive unforced error.
Pen-pushing's easier, I think,
Than teetering on another's brink.
And, yes, to make my mood less dark
I'll play some tennis in the park.

Weeding

Here I am again with my sickle, spade, hoe
To decide over life and death, presume to call
This plant a 'weed', that one a 'flower',
Adam's prerogative, hereditary power
I can't renounce. And yet I know, I know,
It is a single generator drives them all,
And drives my murderous, my ordering hand.

These foxgloves, these red poppies, I let them stand,
Though I did not sow them. Slash the fruit-bearing bramble,
Dig out ground elder, bindweed, stinging nettle,
Real rivals, invaders whose roots ramble,
Robbing or strangling those of more delicate plants.
Or perhaps it's their strength, putting me on my mettle
To fight them for space, resist their advance.

2

I stop. I drop the spade,
Mop my face, consider:
Who's overrun the earth
And almost outrun it?
Who'll make it run out?
Who bores and guts it,
Pollutes and mutates it,
Corrodes and explodes it?
Each leaf that is laid
On the soil will feed it,
Turning death into birth.
If the cycle is breaking
Who brought it about?

I shall go again to the overgrown plot
With my sickle, hoe, spade,
But use no weedkiller, however selective,
No chemicals, no machine.
Already the nettles, ground elder, bindweed
Spring up again.
It's a good fight, as long as neither wins,
There are fruit to pick, unpoisoned,
Weeds to look at. I call them 'wildflowers'.

Psychosis

Where are you, girl, under the whole hulk
Of smooth flesh unused, the figurehead eyes
Pale blue enamel staring, no laughter, no tears
To rise from within against lamplight, daylight
And refract them, playing?
Your lips are composed, for death.
When they part and the life in you finds a word
It is death, it is going down into sleep
And beyond, you're that far away, and there
You look for yourself.
                     I look for you here,
Speak your name, beg you to stay, to wait,
For what, you ask, and I know
With electric currents they tore you
Out of your mad speed,
Joy of a kind, a fury, a pain,
And now with narcotics moor you
To where you are not.
                  Why don't you die, is your answer,
As if there we could meet,
Or else to be rid of me
Trying to hold you, fighting
The undertow, tug of more than your weight
Together with it.
                But where are you,
Where can I reach you with words,
With tongue or finger touch you and make you feel
So that you move again, if only to drift
With the water and winds that are passing you by?

It's your self-love you have lost,
Unloving, and I cannot serve it unloved.
Yet listen for once, tell me
What the place is like where diminished
You long to be less. Let the telling
Cut you loose for your own way.

The Glade

1

All day in the glare, on the salt lake's beaches,
All night in a fever, shaking.
That's done with. My travels are over.
Somehow I'm here: glade in a dense wood.
Leafage makes lace. The shadows are of it, in it,
The season is everymonth.
White sorrel around me, and white anemone,
Foxglove purple, strawberry red.
Apple shapes, pear shapes have lasted all winter.
And the snow gleams above dry moss.

You don't see it, you cannot see it,
Travelling still to a town the guidebook foretells:
How it is to have gone and returned and gone
And returned and forgotten to go
And forgotten the route and the place
And be there again, and be everywhere.

Stay with me, love, till my fingers have traced the landscape
On your body and into your mind.

2

May we lie there, you ask; and how long.
By the hour, for ever, on a bed leased
From the turning trees and the conifers.
Leaving again and again,
Again and again left
To the dark and the whorled light.

Can you bear the silence between us?
You're of it, love, you are in it.
I fondle the silence between us
When I touch you and when I have lost you.

So late, nothing can part us:
We belong to the glade.

70

Mad Lover, Dead Lady

Oh, my Diotima.
Is it not my Diotima you are speaking of?
Thirteen sons she bore me, one of them is Pope,
Sultan the next, the third is the Czar of Russia.
And do you know how it went with her?
Crazy, that's what she went, crazy, crazy, crazy.

Thirteen funerals they gave me when I died.
But she was not there. Locked up in a tower.
That's how it goes: round the bend
Out of the garden where lovers meet,
Walking, talking together. Over the wall.
No one there. Till you visitors come:
Will the corpse write a poem today
About his mad lady?

But I'll tell you a secret: we meet.
Round the bend, on the other side of the wall
Our garden is always there,
Easy, with every season's flowers.
Each from a dark street we come
And the sun shines.
She laughs when I tell her
What it's like to be dead.
I laugh when she gives me
News of our crazy children
Who've made their way in the world.

No poem today, sir.
Go home. In a dream you'll see
How they remove themselves, your dead
Into madness. And seem to forget
Their loved ones, each in his own dark street.
How your mad loved ones
Seem to forget their dead.
That's how it goes. No one there.
Oh, my Diotima.
Waiting for me in the garden.

The Sewing

There was no saying it, you
Found and lost in the time it takes
To open and shut a door,
How every stitch stabbed;
No uttering, crying out
The now, now, now
Without before or after
But what the now could have made.
Had I died there, then,
That would have been true;
Not to mend, as words must,
The break with a thread.

There is no telling it now,
Or ever, to you, though I must
In words that will break again
Only because I live, driving or walking
Through the streets of a different town,
A carrier for coats that need buttons.
And the now is never, never,
The corner passed daily, twice,
With a buttoned coat, to be stabbed,
Far off, the thread loose.

Here's nothing, then: true words
Turned into lies by the lacked act.

Love

It ought to make mystics of us,
This concentration of all that we are and have
On nothing.
But I can't talk. Though my life flowed out to you
In words, while you lay
With another, at peace, happy,
What's ink compared to the juice
Which, more promptly undeceived, I might have spilt
For nothing.

If we must fall into it, for it,
No man was luckier than the near-mystic
Who at eighty-two years
Poured his love out in pints of blood
From the heart, lungs, mouth,
And died on his mistress, in bed,
Before she could leave him
With nothing.

You I write, even now, as though
Having words left, tenderness, folly unspent,
I owed them to you still
And hadn't given enough
To nothing
When happy, at peace in your presence I couldn't know
That had my blood splotched your body, soured the half-lies on
      your lips
Within hours you'd have washed it off, clean and new for another –
Another way of losing yourself
In nothing.

Consumed

The fault was impatience to live, burning,
The fault was joy that flashes and strikes, burning

And made this hollow where now the creature
Hibernates in my heart and guts.
Not that I let it in – I have never seen it.
If it was there from the start
It must have been free to slip out and return,
Feed and breed, run across turf, moss,
Leap or drop from one tree on to another.

Curled up now it sleeps; will twitch, as though dreaming
But not budge. Sustained by its own fat
Retches when I eat, turns every food against me.
What protrudes is my bones. No bulge betrays
How the creature thrives inside me.
Yet women, warned by a handshake, look,
Sense the redundant presence, and keep away.

When spring comes the creature will stir, leave me,
The hollow hurt again, ache to be filled.
Joy will strike again, burning,
And finish me off.

Dust

1

Living with it, till the flakes
Are thick enough to pick up
With my fingers and drop
Into wastepaper basket, bin
Or bowl, whichever is nearest,
Must I recant, take back
My 'hymn to dusters' (unwritten)
Now that she they were meant for dusts
Another man's rooms? A traitor,
In turn, not to her but all
Those heroic housewives, charwomen,
Worldwide relentless army
Fighting the stuff with equipment
So various, intricate, fussy,
It scares me, as dust does not?
Dropped out, for good, from that unending campaign,
Their daily advance by inches,
Their nightly retreat by as many
Or more; the chemical warfare,
The cleaning of cleaning utensils,
Maintenance of the means of maintaining
What never can be maintained.

No, I'll revoke nothing,
Not even revoked love,
Things that dust blurs or dust
Blown away uncovers,
Awed, as before, by the valour
Of grappling till death with death;
But, tainted, feel free to prefer
The smell of dust to the smell
Of disinfectants, polish,
Floorcloth and mop, breathing in
Matter's light breath, exhalation
That mingles pollen with down,
Germs with ashes, and falls
On my brooms, my vacuum cleaner,

On the whiteness of pillow, paper,
Unendingly falls, whirls,
Drifts or settles, fertile
And deadly, like being alive.

2

And yet in a dream I see them,
The dreamers of reason, the cleaners
Humanly march to the coast
Of every ocean on earth
To clear the beaches, reform
Those flotsam-retching waters,
Their seaweed-killer guns
Cocked in the cause of order.

The music I hear, dreaming,
Is canon, fugue, ricercare,
No slop, no loose ends.
If they sing there, under
A cloudless sky, while they let
Pure sand run through their fingers,
The waves hold back, it is:
Veni creator spiritus,
Antibiotic, make us
More than the dust that we are.
Lest we lie too long in bed,
Day-dreaming, of night,
Of nature's way with our flesh,
Come, spirit, and destroy
What merely lives and dies;
Give us the dream of reason.

I wake to the howling of winds.
To darkness. I breathe dust.

Ode to Joy

You're somewhere, they tell me, hiding
Only from me. When I say you've gone, moved out
They show me benches, floors,
Doorsteps, the stone of back yards
You sleep on now. Hint that I may have seen you
And walked by, no eyelash left of your features
To blink recognition and, blinking, be recognized.
Brag that they meet you, know you, have made you
Their mescalin bride, for moments deep and delicate as you
      were
To me when one house could hold you,
One mirror suffice you, one garden was yours
Even in winter, the last of your heelmarks
Blindly divined under snow.

Hide? How can you, so near?
The less he courted you then
The more you amazed your long-faced lover
Come from his black pudding dinner, his raventail party
Down streets where the lamps had failed, by being there,
Waiting in candlelight, faithful to him.
Could leave for a sunny country, lock up,
Write him no postcard for weeks, for a month or longer
And return with a present, unchanged.
He, for the shareholders, meanwhile had itemized that year's
      trading losses,
Balanced their total against the depreciation of assets
And declared a minus dividend –
Coolly lugubrious. He could count on you.

All right. We're older. The dirtier air
Blocks or thickens the waves you transmitted.
Computers will plot a course
For the homing of homeless migrants,
The wildflowers you looked for will blossom on paper.
But call on me once, as different as you like,
As briefly, casually. Caring so little now
Where you are, with whom, you will hardly notice

What strangers we have become. We need not talk
If I hear you breathe in this room, this world,
Light finds a shape to outline,
A body to shine on, to shade.

Gone

Thomas Good: born Beeston, Notts., 29 October 1901
missing from Richmond, Surrey, since 20 January 1970

1

"The presence of 200 guests,
Many of them only waiting
To die, depresses me.
I have not had the strength
To go to London. But
I hope to leave
After the 15th of January.
If I remember rightly,
February is like
A little springtime.
The other plans
I shall put off
Till April."
                     My luggage
Has failed me here
Against a room worn
As my clothes, my books,
Manuscripts thumbed
By indifferent men
And returned. How long, how far
I have shifted them
Across the frontiers, decades
Only to bring them here,
Home, Terminus Hall
Where no one dances
To penny whistle or gramophone,
A decorous quiet obtains
And the wallpaper, worn,
Repeats in weary tones
Its admonition:
                     Rest.
Give up your journeys,
Give up your jumbled loves,
Lady of Pimlico,

79

Lady of Beirut
Who in Oxford and Aix and Verona and everywhere
Smiled from a bus,
Nodded high on a horse
As you fluttered on
With your phrases picked
From an earlier dawn's adoration,
Skipped with a joy
Your churchy youth forbade,
When the coin was valid.
Well, yes. I spent my life leaping
From memories to plans,
From loss to recollection.
This room clamps me
To the empty space between...

2

Once more he packed. With meticulous care
Though his mind was wandering out to the streets of wintry
    London,
Loitering on doorsteps of houses demolished by bombs,
Faltering over doorbells that no one he knew could answer,
North, by the Midlands, to Filey "surrounded by landscapes
That enchant me more and more", south again to Sussex,
And over Channel, rivers, mountains, Mediterranean sea,
While his hands disposed
Diary, wallet, passport, tobacco tin filled with coins,
Things he had done with. Paid his rent to the day,
Put on his raincoat and beret, walked out,
Leaving all he possessed, and one library book, overdue.

3

Feeling that void grow
Best filled with earth,
In old age or sickness a cat
From house to thicket will drag it,
Under a laurel hedge, close
To the roots will sit,

Nothing more in her gaze
Than a meek waiting,
Alone with it and the air's
Hummed continuum
Ever the same, from birth.

Could he, tunes in his head,
Busoni, music-hall,
Words in his head,
Heard and read,
Lie down or fall, hide
From eyes inside him
Of his living, his dead?
To what earth, what water, where
In a city not pitiless
Creep into animal time
Unowned, untenanted?

4

"There is hardly a climate in England
That suits me; and where to settle
I have not the least idea.
I am not allowed
To draw my pension abroad."
And yet, to keep moving,
Mind and body at one
Till mind stops, body drops
Is freedom of a kind.
I cannot help it, this joy
That gathers me up to defy
The better judgement of walls,
Gathers all I have been,
All I have loved, and drives me
I don't know where, to rest,
I don't know where, to die.

Thames

Good river, it carries
Food for men, for gulls.

Beautiful river
This winter evening
It melts into mauves and greys
Tower, chimney, wharf,
A mirror breathed upon
By haze and the lips of lovers.

This afternoon I saw
My friend's face, purple
After forty days of drifting
Between cold banks, in the brown water;

And drove home, along
The Embankment where he
Had breathed, loitered, loved
In a haze, mauves and greys
While the refuse of gulls, of men
Slapped the black bulk of barges.

White-faced, but with fuel enough,
With food enough to keep going
Today, tomorrow not far from the river,
Still able at times to be fooled,

Down through the rippled lamplight
I drive, into real mud.

Roses, Chrysanthemums

It's late in the day, in the year,
The frost holding off, just.
In the garden you pick dry stalks, hardly looking.
Time to come in,
Time to pick flowers, only now,
And carry them in, summer and autumn bunched,
Toward winter, even the full roses' petals
In no hurry to fall.

It is a slow music we hear
Behind the wind. And the chrysanthemums
Are a slow fire,
A red so dark it glimmers and would go out
But for the yellow that radiates from the core.
Ruffled flutterings here, a harsh odour
As of wood-smoke, and there
Flesh colour, silky, taut in its bland breathing,
Linger and mingle.

Now. Only now.

'Berkshire's Ancient Man'
For Richard

1

He can't be walking there now,
His head, bird-like, stuck out,
Ever so slightly tilted
Not for looking askance
At the new housing estate,
Not for looking at all
At the changes, mattresses dumped
In the ditches along the lane,
Nor stopping, except to roll
A fag or, for less than a minute,
Chat with us, chuckle
Over the rare good luck
Of having survived so long,
Outlived his wife, his acquaintance
And his very calling of coachman.
Cars didn't bother him.
No, horses it was
Had done for his father, his brother,
His father's father before them,
All coachmen or grooms in their time.

Suppose that his luck held,
The lane is a lane still,
No car knocked him down:
Near-centenarian then,
A decade ago and more,
He can't be walking there now.

2

At the southern end of the Appalachians,
Walking in autumn, in failing light
Up the narrow trail to the Horseshoe Falls
And meeting horses, climbing a bank
To let them pass, I remembered him

And the name you gave him, a child,
In a poem I lost or mixed up
With other papers that may or may not
Be somewhere in boxes no one is likely
To look at till both of us have forgotten
The old man of Berkshire. Already
The memory of that remembering fades out
In evening light, the shapes of leaves
On the trail, the waterfall high up
In the rocks, and the horses, passing.
Such distances lie between. We do not walk
Down the lane from village to village,
Suburbs by now, nor shall again.
So, for less than a minute, let
Him walk there still, your childhood poem
Be found, and even the half-lit trail
Three thousand miles away, never seen
By you, connect with the old man
Wickedly chuckling over the luck
Of having tricked them, those deadly horses.

Gardening

I

Most of the time it's enough
That a green tip shows,
Confirming you in the freedom to see
The flowering due next year.
Even the bare patch, undug,
Could be feeding
Slow lily bulbs
You gave up for dead.
If buds appear
Be alert, lest you're looking the other way
When anticipation, met or surpassed,
Becomes void for an hour, a day,
For a whole week.
Novelties are not new,
Unless it was bird, wind
That brought the seed;
And finally
You may cease to mind
Whether of currant, yew,
The neighbour's columbine
Or common weed –
As long as it grows.
Nothing's unique
But sunbeam's, light's play
On leafage foreknown.
That keeps you working, waiting –
That and the need
For what you think you are bored by:
For continuity,
A place of your own
Where bird, wind passes through.

II

Ripeness is all; but
The apples and pears that last
Take longest to ripen.
This early pear
Turns mushy or mealy one day
After it's ripe.
And the earliest fruit to ripen
Is the one with a maggot
Busy inside, at the core.

To be slow, to take time
And what the sun has to give,
Not to fall
In late summer, in autumn gale,
Ripening, is all.

Real Estate

For Anne

1

Weary we came to it, weary
With advertisement's weary verbiage
And all those inglenooks, plastic antiquities,
The cocktail bar cottage,
The swimming-pool farmhouse,
The concreted paddocks, the pink mirrors lining
That bathroom suite in the Georgian mansion,
All the stuff that, bought at a steep price,
We could never afford to get rid of, by de-converting.

2

'For sale by auction: The Rectory,
Standing in well-timbered grounds
In this unspoilt village.
A fine period house requiring
Improvement and restoration.
A range of Outbuildings.' Yes.
'A Garage'. Noted.

3

We went. And there it stood,
Plain, white, right,
Austere, but with gables, bow front
('A later addition'), hint
Of indulgence in curves, dips.
Large, but not grand, compact.
Too sure of itself to be showy.
So real, it amazed, overwhelmed you.
So self-sufficient, you wanted it.

4

For sale by auction, at a low reserve,
After Easter, the powerful temptation
Of realness, every inch of the house honest –
With the rendering brutally stripped
Here and there, to reveal
Rot of beams, erosion, cracks
In brick, stone, the sliding,
Minute even now, and slow, slow,
Down into older dampness, of the foundations.

5

Settle there, could you, dare you,
On settlement? Settle ('subject to covenant'),
Bid for a place become
Pure idea of duration, dwelling
Among rook caws up in the black yews,
The taller pines, near graves,
Near enough to feel always
Held there, beyond dislodging –
If the floorboards, only a little aslant,
Hold, if the roof holds, if . . .

6

And the gardens, wilderness
Whose high walls keep intact
The pure idea, *hortus conclusus*,
Her who reigned with her lilies
Over wilderness trained, restrained –
Graveyard, no more, true
For bough, blossom, fruit
Gone down into older dampness,
To rise again, fleshed, if . . .

If not, the dead in their graves,
Near enough, will be heard laughing
At folk who need so much room,
Such an effort of warmed walls,
To make a home for themselves, a peace;
And on their treetops the rooks
Join in, with a raucous guffawing.

Let's go, let the place be:
Too real for us to meddle with, pure idea of dwelling.
Not for us will the rooks caw
Or the gardens bear again flowers and fruit;
Not at us will the rooks laugh.
But anywhere, miles from this burial-ground,
The wide-awake dead can tell us a thing or two
About making do with our real estate,
The for ever indifferently furnished, poorly maintained,
Defectively fenced or walled;
About how indifference grows on us, and the chores grow harder.

9

Let's go, and revisit those empty rooms,
Occupy them in dreams that restore without labour
Any house you have lost
Or lacked the means to acquire; improve it, too.
One look, and dream takes possession
Of all that the look took in; and will work wonders
With ruins, with rubble, with the bare site,
Instantly will rebuild, instantly raise the dead
For conversation with you, for communion;
And where no root is, no seed,
Break sunbeams for you with the blackness of full-grown pines.

View from a Back Window
Bay State Road, Boston

A strip of street where nobody walks,
Cars, between dustbins, illegally park
('Police take notice'), fenced for safety
With concrete, wire, against the two-way flow
Of traffic on the throughway. Then,
Unfenced, the grassy bank, with trees, a path
Where nobody walks but joggers run.
Still closer to the wide dividing waters
That hardly seem to flow, their surface ripple
Flattened, slowed down by trucks, a bench more green
Than the short grass it stands on. There
A man – voyeur of beer cans, eavesdropper
On engine rumble, chassis rattle, screech
Of tires, gratuitous inhaler
Of gases not his property – could sit
And, willing, strong enough to raise his eyes
On the far bank observe the two-way flow
Of traffic on the throughway; then
The tall façades, bare tenement, turret of château,
Factory chimney, mosque rotunda, where
Behind the blocked view seeing could begin.

At Staufen

For Peter Huchel

1

"Too tame, too pretty", you said,
Sitting in front of your borrowed villa
Overlooking vineyards, the wide plain
That far off, when the haze lifts,
Outlines the Vosges;
Or, if you turned your head,
Closer, the mountainous fringe
Of the forest they call black.

Not black enough, for you,
Driven out of your true home,
The menaced, the menacing East?
Tamed for timber, tended,
Its nature trails
Pedagogically furnished
With the names and provenance
Of representative trees;
And the foxes gone,
Gassed, for fear of rabies.

Not black enough, for you,
On their hill, the castle ruins
Pedagogically preserved
With a plaque for Faust?

2

Yet the homeless cats,
Untouchable, gone wild,
Came to you for food,
One of them dragging
A leg ripped by shot.
Above the swimming pool
Buzzards hung, cried.
High up, from a tree-top

92

An oriole slid
Through its small range of tones
And once, once only
Flashed in quick flight,
Making oak, ash, fir
Look blacker.

Nor would you let
Ladybirds, butterflies
Drown, or be gutted alive
By the black water beetle
That ruled the pool.

Too late I skimmed off
A golden gardener,
And returned to my book,
Old-fashioned Fabre's
'Social Life in the Insect World'.
To find that very species
Observed, recorded there:
Its mass killing
Of caterpillars,
The female's nuptial feast
On the male.

I closed the book,
And kept the corpse
For the green and gold of its wings.

3

Dark the gravestones were, too,
At Sulzburg, the Hebrew letters
Blacked out by centuries
Of moss on the oldest;
With no new ones to come,
With the last of a long line
Gassed, east of here, gone.

Well tended, fenced off
From the camping ground
And the forest's encroachment,
That site was black enough
Even where sunbeams lit
New leaves, white flowers.

You said nothing, looking:
Slabs of stone, lettered or blank,
Stuck into black loam.
The names that remained, German;
The later inscriptions, German;
No stone, no inscription
For the last of the line,
Who were carrion, Jewish.

4

Yes, much blacker they'll be,
Much bleaker, our landscapes, before
'Desert is our history,
Termites with their pincers
Write it
On sand.'

But with eyes that long have stared
Into the dark, seeing,
You can look still
At the vineyards, the forest's edge
Where even now
A pine-marten kills, as it must,
Wild or tame prey;

Still can feed
The homeless cats,
Can save, as you must,
From natural, from
Man-made death
Insects that, brilliant or drab,
Are skilled, fulfilled in killing
And willing, in turn, to be killed;

94

Can write, still, write
For the killers, the savers
While they survive.
For the termites, eaters
Of paper, while they survive.
Or the sand alone,
For the blank sand.

Mornings

String of beginnings, a lifetime long,
So thin, so strong, it's outlasted the bulk it bound,
Whenever light out of haze lifted
Scarred masonry, marred wood
As a mother her child from the cot,
To strip, to wash, to dress again,
And the cities even were innocent.
In winter too, if the sun glinted
On ice, on snow,
Early air was the more unbreathed
For being cold, the factory smoke
Straighter, compact, not lingering, mingling.
I look at the river. It shines, it shines
As though the banks were not littered
With bottles, cans, rags
Nor lapped by detergents, by sewage,
Only the light were true.
I look at light: but for them, mornings,
Every rising's not-yet,
Little remains now to wait for, wish for,
To praise, once the shapes have set;
And whatever the end of my days, to the last
It will hold, the string of beginnings,
Light that was, that will be, that is new.

Conversations with Charwomen

1

If I'd spent my life alone
Or had my way in such matters
They'd never have taken place.
Irreversibly bourgeois,
Heir to the title deeds
Of an abyss impalpable and luxurious
As a gold mine in Peru
Which no broker can sell,
Nonetheless I've always preferred
To do my own dirty work,
Loath to call upon
Charwoman, charlady, cleaning lady,
Domestic help, auxiliary household fairy,
Madonna of mops, demi-goddess of buckets.
To do? Not quite: more often to leave undone –
Preoccupied with 'higher things', as they once would have called
My inheritance, the abyss, and the lifelong bother
Of trying in vain to get rid of it.

2

Well, they took place,
Those distracting conversations
About cleaning materials more strange to me
Than my unspeakable property
Could have been to her who was widowed,
Her who brought a small daughter,
Her with arthritis, whom it hurt to see on her knees,
And over and over again
About tea, strong or weak, Indian or China,
About biscuits, buns, cake,
Where obtainable, being delicious,
About the weather I had been too busy
To taste for myself.

So distracted I grew, so distraught,
One morning I nearly cried out:
Woman, where's yours? I mean your abyss.
Where is it? And how can I learn
To mislay it, as you do, for hours at a stretch,
For days, for weeks, for months,
For the decade or two we have left?
And how, while our capital rots,
Learn to believe in pennies?

Frothy questions. Each one of those women
With her work and her words refuted them.
Besides, the abyss is private
And the last thing I can afford
Is to lose my self-possession.
So: That's right, Mrs Williams, I agreed yet again,
There's no doubting that tea contains tannin,
A stimulant, a drug, if you like, a poison.
But it does cheer us up, as you say.

Mr Littlejoy

I

Mr Littlejoy rises on a May morning
To feed his pondfish, then his treefrog. His?
Nothing is yours, the weather says. Amen.
The showery season makes them rise to eat.

Sunbeams today. A dry sun-worshipper
He blesses dry fish food, then earthworm, fly
For being up and going down. Amen.
Small food for the small creatures in his tending.

Wind. Broken cloud. What is, is all there is,
The weather says, and he believes the weather.
Now scales flash golden. Later, blur. Amen.
This frog's purveyor will be food for worms

Or smaller creatures, he hears the weather say;
And, good, has learnt to answer back. Amen.

II

Mid-day is past. Mid-week, mid-month, mid-year.
Three quarters gone the century. Past long ago
My life's mid-way. (Dark forest? No. Bright city,
Open, abuzz, her wound, her stumps on show.)
And the millennium slimes towards its end,

Mr Littlejoy laughs, and prompts himself: laugh now,
As long as lungs dilate and lips will part.
(Something adhesive – lava or miasma –
Prepares to break worn casing. Laugh while you can.
Breathe while you can. And while you breathe, complain.

Still the dreams come. Still in the dog-day drought
This bush puts out true roses, one or two,
Though mildew films the leafage, ladybirds
Cluster a gashed and fallen pear, to drink.
How hope holds on – fungus to rotten wood!

Dreams of renewal, reconciliation:
The estranged friend back, with projects, fantasies
Unpacked, spread out for you, as though for sharing!
A child consults you. A child confides to you,
The dreamer of that child, dreams that were yours.

He dances, dances over the withered lawn.

III

The sea, the sea, oh, to make friends with the sea,
Longs Mr Littlejoy, walking the wide salt marshes
Towards winter, at low tide. The hungry gulls
Above him circle, shriek as he prods a cluster
Of prickly oysters, picks the largest, bags it,
Walks on with care yet crunches underfoot
Mussels marooned in grasses, winkles attached
To sandbank, rock, then plunges a cold arm
Into the slime of a pool's bed, groping for clams.
That underground is depleted. He tries again,
Pool after pool, in vain. Plods on. The near gulls cry.
Peculiar gases rise. He stops, plods on,
But to his ankles, to his knees, no, to his waist
Sinks into mud that gurgles at him, holds him,
So fondly sucks at him, he feels, he knows:
The sea accepts me. I've made friends with the sea.
And, stuck there, seems to hear a siren song,
The moan of whales, as caught, as taped by his kind
On their kind's way across depleted waters:
Cow's call to calf, cow's call to slaughtered bull.
Whole cities the soft mire of bog, he marvels,
Fenland supports that drags one lean man down.
The sea, the sea makes me a monument,
Memorial founded on the wide salt marshes
To the sea's friend, recorder of her whales.

100

Post Mortem

For Thomas Blackburn

1

Four nights without sleep in his mountain cottage,
Four nights of climbing
Clear of the humus where roots
Grapple and feed and rot.

Four nights of writing himself
Clean into death;
And deftly managing, timing
A last intensity
To leave no loathed loose ends.
Bare rock-face, sheer.

All went to plan.
He'd finished the final draft
Of his tricky last chapter,
Transmuting the bitterness, blame.
Now verse, for valediction,
Thanksgiving, blessing,
His 'Morituri':
Not in his chatty manner
But songlike once more, taut.
And finished that before
The drug blasted his brain,
He groaned and rose and lurched,
Reeled once, collapsed.

2

Hadn't he noticed? There was a line
Missing. Couldn't he find a rhyme,
Or only a half-rhyme, for 'suffer'?
Did his climb go wrong after all,
The rope snap as he fumbled
At the ledge he'd picked for his fall?

He never was neat, my old friend.
Too late, too late I could offer
Full rhymes, half-rhymes enough,
As decades ago I would
When he sent me his scrawls,
Who was gruffer, rougher by far
Than he could bear to be
And made himself, for the end.
That marred the symmetry,
That blocked the fulfilling echo:
How he willed his way of dying,
Forced and bent his verse
Into a gentleness, grimly,
Into a brightness, darkly.

In the flaw lies the rightness,
What he could not will, but was,
On the slopes, among scrub and scree.
And there I can see him, there.

Let 'suffer' hang in the air.

Birthday

A shovel scrapes over stone or concrete.
Cars drone. A child's voice rises
Above the hubbub of nameless play.

An afternoon in August. I lie drowsing
On the garden bench. Fifty years melt
In the hot air that transmits
The sounds of happenings whose place and nature
Hang there, hover. That's how it was
For the baby laid down on a balcony
At siesta time in a distant city;
And is here, now. The known and the seen
Fall away. A space opens,
Fills with the hum, the thrumming of what
I am not; the screams, too, the screeching;
Becomes the sum of my life, a home
I cannot inhabit – with the sparrows even
Mute this month, all commotion human.

Elsewhere, my mother at eighty-eight
Lies on a deck chair, drowning
In that same space. Were my father alive
Today he'd be ninety, the tissue
Undone in him larger by thirty-five years;
But the sounds and the silence round him
The same; here, to receive him, the space.

A train rattles by. A drill, far off,
Throbs. A cup falls, shatters.

At Home

For my mother, at the age of 90

Early June. In a heatwave London is loosened.
Over fences, brick walls grown lighter
Wandering tendrils play.
Tourists are out, adrift, briefly to live by looking.

You're there; and your eyes can see:
Shapes you have handled, features the years have sharpened.
Your gaze cannot hold them for long. They will not stay,
Tugged away from you – into what?
A duration like music's you enter and leave, estranged.

You're there, but not in your garden.
Wisteria fragrance
Blows in through french windows half-open.
No need to rise from your bed or your chair:

Without looking you know how the weeds are taking over,
The last of your gardeners gone;
How convolvulus buds on the smothered gooseberry bushes
And soon will blatantly flower.

Still disorder hurts you. Your body, by hurting more,
Tells you each day to let go.
And the house, too, withdraws from your rule and possession.

Things have been shifted. If now you recall and wonder
Where it might be, your grandmother's tablecloth –
So devoutly embroidered and fringed
That all those decades devoutly you must preserve it –
For the giving away you summon the ghost of a care.

London, limbered or cold, has changed and receded:
In districts you cannot envisage your grandchildren lodge.
Yet they come to you; and you're there,
And can see them and listen – till their voices drop out of your
    time;

104

Into what? – A movement like music's
That reaching out to its limits arrives there only
To rest at the home of its range.

And that's where you are – your smile alone will concede it –
While, beyond you, your house dissolves.

A Silence
In Memoriam L.M.H., 1887-1980

I

The mellow light once more: late August.
Mat light on a fulness of leaves
About to die back, and a few slow flowers
She's finished with now but, newly widowed, saw
Four decades ago, in a different garden,
A street war had emptied;
And again and again before
She gave in at last, going
Between night and daybreak, between
Two anniversaries,
Of widowhood, wedding.

Little her care could maintain but the flowers' recurrence.
Nor that much, when last
She sat in her garden, looking
Past care at the flowerbeds, changed
In recurrent light, estranged;
And could not, would not see
Her fruit trees lopped down
To the bare trunks, all their branchwork heaped
In the farthest corner, for burning.
The light it was that remained, only the light.

II

"Take me home, let me go home",
She demanded, implored on her chair,
Her bed, in the same room
That was drifting now in a time-stream
Reversed, away, away.
Or set out in mind
For a party thrown for her by the past,
With Mama and Papa there
To save her at last from the hostess,
A psychiatrist who had picked on her,

Wouldn't let her leave,
Probed with impertinent questions.
"Naughty girl", said the nurse,
Removing her telephone
When she reached out to ring
The house that was truly hers,
The other house down the street
With the other bed, hers truly,
That waited there, never used
But made up, for rest.

Yet grief was falling away,
Anger could grip nothing,
So helpless she was, even love
Must turn back, to the root
And, far from the limbs, lie dormant.
What remained was laughter, driven through pain,
In a gasp she could prove herself:
Laughing at love that could do nothing,
That must give up at last, go.

III

Dial the number of her locked house
Where the brick holds,
Leaves breathe, roots drink;
And silences opened, the room rang hollow
Between reassurances then,
As by millimetres she slid
Off the thin wire on which alone
Bravely she'd poised a presence.

Dial the number and listen, listen:
To the hum or buzz, the high or low,
Broken, unbroken tone
Used, as words were,
Against silence, the gist, the gist.
Meet there again, where beginnings meet their ends,
Ends their beginnings, to diverge is to follow.
Listen, and never tell.

Willow

Hard wood or soft?
It is light, startlingly,
Not close-grained, to last
As oak does; but makes up
In obstinate wiry toughness for that
With all its fibres.
From the barkless bough
My axe rebounds;
My handsaw bends,
From the sham death
Willow, by shamming, defies.

Pick any twig, dormant
Or wrenched off in a gale,
Stick it in moist earth,
And it makes a tree.
Leave a trunk, fallen
Or felled, sprawling
Across a stream,
And it lives on,
Sprouts from the hollow
Half-rotten stump or
Takes root from a dropped limb.

Chop up the dry remains,
Burn them: they'll spit.

Birch

Vestal she seems, ballerina
Of wildest, of waste places,
With an aspiration to whiteness
Fulfilled in America's North,
A papery peel so flawless,
It would shame the contagion of ink;
Yet rarely will attain
Her maturity's fulness,
Too often herself wasted,
Her bitter, her harsh timber
Stunted by what she favours,
Blizzards bending her limbs,
Long stillness under snow;
Will lie prone suddenly,
Crowded out, or as though felled
By a blow from her own boughs.
And proves brittle then, graceless:
Her wrappings of bark more lasting
Than the mouldered body within.

Yew

Too slowly for us it amasses
Its dense dark bulk.
Even without our blood
For food, where mature one stands
It's beyond us, putting on
Half-inches towards its millennium,
Reaching down farther
Than our memories, our machines.
Its fertile berries can kill.
Its dead wood even, still harsh,
In gate-post or bedstead
Outlasts many users
Of gates, of beds.
Woodworm, bedbug avoid it,
Those who used it said.

If one tree stands, black,
Where many trees were
And they whose counter-nature
For all things had a use
Till unburied their flesh littered
The used, the flayed earth,
A yew it will be, split,
Thrusting down slow roots,
Millennial, still to where
Soil remains whole.

Balsam Poplar

As a sucker, mere stick, awry,
This one was found and uprooted,
Took to the place, and within five years,
True, straight, it has risen
Not at the rate of the Lombardy
Whose one aspiration is to become
A landmark, leaving the slower oaks
To compete for breath, dwarfed as cottages are
By the church spire; but puts out instead
Lateral boughs, leafage larger and longer
Which, in bud and new, exhales
A jonquil sweetness, as though
It needed no flowers to fulfil itself,
Sterile perhaps, until
The roots, mature, can provide for offspring.

So fragrant, it seems exotic,
Yet after a winter that killed and lingered
Is more forthcoming than its more common kin,
The white and the black, still bare;
Sturdier, too, in its fibre and shape,
Lets go of no branch or leaf
In a gale, nor jitters like aspen.

Never yet having gathered
One fallen twig, for burning,
Nor lopped or chopped its timber,
I cannot tell where the sweetness begins,
Whether in wood cells, engrained,
Whether distilled out of acrid earth
Or only at the tips, by a marriage with air.

Oak

Slow in growth, late in putting out leaves,
And the full leaves dark, austere,
Neither the flower nor the fruit sweet
Save to the harsh jay's tongue, squirrel's and boar's,
Oak has an earthward urge, each bough dithers,
Now rising, now jerked aside, twisted back,
Only the bulk of the lower trunk keeps
A straight course, only the massed foliage together
Rounds a shape out of knots and zigzags.

But when other trees, even the late-leaved ash,
Slow-growing walnut, wide-branching beech and linden
Sway in a summer wind, poplar and willow bend,
Oak alone looks compact, in a stillness hides
Black stumps of limbs that blight or blast bared;
And for death reserves its more durable substance.

On wide floorboards four centuries old,
Sloping, yet scarcely worn, I can walk
And in words not oaken, those of my time, diminished,
Mark them that never were a monument
But plain utility, and mark the diminution,
Loss of that patient tree, loss of the skills
That matched the patience, shaping hard wood
To outlast the worker and outlast the user;
How by oak beams, worm-eaten,
This cottage stands, when brick and plaster have crumbled,
In casements of oak the leaded panes rest
Where new frames, new doors, mere deal, again and again have
    rotted.

Elder

Tree-sized weed that, allowed to prosper,
Will impersonate ash
From a distance at least
And in leaf only, before
It puts on blossom or berry,
A blushing white or a blackish crimson
From its imposture of branches
Whose marrow is pith, or nothing,
With a weed's impudence elder,
Bird-seeded, will crop up
Anywhere, useful to birds
As to human consumers able,
By fermentation, to draw
From the dry flowers, acrid pulp of the fruit
An essence pungently sweet.

Such use it permits
But punishes those
Taken in by its would-be timber
To burn it indoors.
I did, and learned:
Taken in, for burning,
One felled intruder yielded
Little brightness, less heat.
Worse, my favourite pipe
Dropped for no reason, the stem,
Hollow too, not of good wood either,
Irreparably snapped.

Call it shrub, then, or scrub
Where too rankly it upstarts,
But give it room, if you can,
For a lavish pretending,
For a wealth of moon umbels
Darkening, waning through purple to black.

Winter Jasmine

For a cold blossoming, less than cold praise:
Under veiled skies, in greyness
Eyes too are veiled,
And invisible almost against
A wall too much haze cast adrift
Nor weighty with fragrance as
Of its white kin
Or winter-white viburnum, honeysuckle,
To an absence of bees
It lavishly opens, displays
All those mock-suns, in vain;
Shines, but for senses dormant
Till aconite
With surprise caps its yellow
That fades now, dies.

Winter Aconite, Adonis

Not ostentatious either, long before
The trumpeted daffodils
Make spring official, but so small
That one must know the patch, clear it of sodden grass
To see the curled stalks bear
Furled yellow into still forbidding air
Of this last January day,
Opening only when the sun gets through
Or never, should the drizzle and the mist
Forbiddingly persist.
Furled or unfurled, foreknown or unforeknown,
By sheer anachronism more they will surprise
Than snowdrop white that's wintry to our eyes;
And before snowdrops may have come and gone –

Unlike adonis, built to last, defy
All sorts of weather, by holding back
The sturdier blossom on the sturdier stalk
For weeks, or months if need be, cunningly,
Leafage wrapped round it, and a tinge of green
Outside the yellow petals, for disguise,
Unfurling, furling, till true warmth sets in.
Then let the fanfares blare,
The pampered pomp of frilly daffodils blaze!
Its work is done, in frost's and wind's despite,
To put on death now, sweet
While all and sundry feast on the easier air.

Winter Honeysuckle

i.m. Elizabeth Smart

White as hoarfrost, whiter than ice,
In hoarfrost, ice its floweret petals open
For what angelic bees to pollinate –
Night-flying bees, inaudible and white?
As though white-pillowed in white sheets, and white
Not only smiling a dead face could lie
But take and leave no break,
No season's growth retracted, not one day disowned.
Nor, in snow flurries, leafless:
Fragrant from shoots all fleshed and newly spread despite
Air that seems deathly too, deep-frozen ground.

Adamic

For David Gascoyne

1

Take your scythe to the flowering grasses
That winds bend, sunbeams wither,
And make a breathing-space for saplings,
For the fruit lately set on low boughs
Of cordon, bush the tall grass would smother,
Bindweed entwine and blight reach unseen.
The year's order it is, yours to uphold,
Salt of the earth, the choice is your own:
Relish the salt on your lip.

2

I go out and lay the good seedheads flat.
There's ease in the motion, both arms obey.
How else could I know the winds, feel the sun?
But more sure than scythe-blade the seasons rip
Through grass-blade and fruit and flesh of the grower.
Hardly he savours the crop he labours to eat,
Eats to labour again. Let up,
Law, for once, let one eye meet one flower
Long enough to see.

3

Now indoors, in halflight, a denser swathe
I cut, all time's growth goes down.
Soon sleep will begin to dig the garden inside me,
So deeply, no root remains but the tree's,
The first, last, all my work's undone.
Though seeing too well I awake, weary,
And rise aware of the bone-bare trunk.
Take your sickle to spurge, to thistle
The order will urge again.

Garden, Wilderness

Green fingers, green hand, by now green man
All through, with sap for blood,
Menial to it, gross nature,
And governor of a green tribe
No law can tame, no equity can bend
From the sole need of each, to feed and seed,
Unless, refined beyond resistance to a blight
More grasping than their greed,
Rare shoots evade the keeper's pampering.

He goes to referee
A clinch of lupin, bindweed, common cleavers
And stinging nettle – each with a right to be
Where if one thrives the other three must weaken;
And with his green hand, kin to tendril, root,
Tugs at the wrestlers, to save, to separate
Although his green heart knows:
While sun and rain connive,
Such will the game remain, such his and their estate.

More rain than sunshine: his green lungs inhale
Air thick with horsetail spore,
Grass pollen; his legs trail
Trains of torn herbage, dragging through swollen growth
Twined, tangled with decay.
For his green food he gropes,
To taste his share, bonus of fruit and berry,
Tribute for regency,
Sweet compensation for defeated hopes
Or dole despite the drudgery, the waste.

A garden of the mind,
Pure order, equipoise and paradigm
His lord, long far away and silent, had designed,
With bodies, never his, indifferent machines
To impose it and maintain

Against the clinging strand, the clogging slime;
And best invisible, as now that lord's become
Whose ghost the green man serves; that contemplated flower
Whose day of stillness filled all space, all time.

Pré-Alpes
For André du Bouchet

1

Fore-alps I understood but meadow-alps we walked,
Lush with the many-shaped, the many-coloured clovers,
Vetches and marguerites, confusion of orchid kinds
And at the ryefield verges a foretime marriage
Of purest blue with scarlet, cornflower and poppy,
Though the wild sage could summon a still deeper blue,
Golden-eyed white was sweetest, gave out the heaviest fragrance
When wind or breeze ran loose among narcissus heads:
Persephone's meadows no farmer can quite possess.
His little herd or flock may crop the flora moist,
In winter munch the essences held in hay,
But mountainside, fallen rock, ravine where the spring waters
Creep through low leafage, gurgling, gather or cascade
Keep the man frugal, his narrow pastures rich,
Wildflowers outshone, outglittered by the wings of beetle,
Daymoth and butterfly, stone by the emerald lizard,
The copses loud with nightingales, roadside with cricket,
Sky with the buzzard's mew – in bird-murdering France –
Even the grass snake from the legend it will be,
If any legend can outlive the legend-bearers,

2

Last of these farmer-builders holding out
Against the silence of rooms too large
Under the vaulted or the timbered ceiling,
Too cool, too dark in summer
Under the triple pantiles of the roof
In homesteads long cast adrift
From villages that are names now,
Their workshops, stores, cafés
Closed down, the women gone;
And, hacking at sun-baked clay
For survival without succession –
No child's voice to be heard

120

From house or pasture or track –
On another hillside can see
A homestead's half-ruin
Abandoned by one who lies,
Unvisited even there,
In his walled family graveyard
Where, black, a great cypress
Lives on, not felled yet
By the land's new owners,
Indifferent city folk;
One who could not wait
Till old age imposed a truce
With nature, let him go down
In peace, because he must;
But cursing the grim love
That had kept him there, a loser,
The stubborn strength, his undoing,
With a shot broke the silence.

A Painter Painted
Lucian Freud: Francis Bacon (1952)

Portrait or nature morte or landscape (nature vivante) –
Pencil and brush make all a still life, fixed,
So that the wind that swept, breath that came hard
Or easy, when wind has dropped, breath has passed on,
The never visible, may stir again in stillness.

Visible both, the painter and the painted
Passed by me, four decades ago. We met,
We talked, we drank, and we went our ways.
This head's more true than the head I saw.
Closed, these lips tell me more than the lips that spoke.
Lowered, these eyes are better at looking.

A likeness caught? No. Pictor invenit.
Slowly, slowly, under his lowered eyelids
He worked, against time, to find the face grown truer,
Coax it to life in paint's dead millimetres,
Compose them into nature, in a light
That is not London's, any hour's or year's;

Furrow it, too, with darkness; let in the winds
That left their roads, painter's and painted's, littered,
Brought branches down, scattering feathers, fruit,
Though for a moment only, stopped the bland flow of breath.

And here it hangs, the still life of a head.

To Bridge a Lull

i.m. George Oppen

Alone in your genus, ectopistes,
Your flocks were thunder clouds
That discharged themselves on forests,
Clattering down, breaking thick branches
With the weight of your roosts or nests
When you broke your journeys, rested.
In thousands then you were slaughtered,
Smoked out with sulphur, clubbed
Or shot on acres white
With your acid dung. So many
That herds of pigs were turned loose
To fatten on carcasses left
When their keepers, Indian, colonist,
Had bagged all they could eat.
At a mile a minute, billionfold,
Long-tailed and purple-necked,
Powerful flyers, you travelled
Between Mexico and Quebec,
Able to rear, it was thought,
At any season, wherever
Abundance of fruit or seed
Matched your multiple hunger,
One male, one female, and those
Mature within half a year.
And then you were gone;
And then in tens, not thousands
Were seen again and counted;
And then were not seen again.

Ectopistes. Vagrants. A dead name I write
To bridge a lull. Absurdly let
Lips, tongue that will be dumb
Address what is not, never could make out
The spoken or the written vocable, dead.
And hear the clatter still,
Come down to ravage forests razed
By your self-ravaging destroyers

123

Whose obsolescent words I write.
And see the sky blacked out
Not where your millions passed,
Light breaking as you hurtled to escape
Eagle or hawk, armed with their talons only,
But by a larger, lingering darkness that's unbroken.
A stillness, cold, your kind could share with mine
Fills with your flocks, absurdly
Brings back what dead men called you, passenger.

from *Variations*

Travelling I

1

Mountains, lakes. I have been here before
And on other mountains, wooded
Or rocky, smelling of thyme.
Lakes from whose beds they pulled
The giant catfish, for food,
Larger, deeper lakes that washed up
Dead carp and mussel shells, pearly or pink.
Forests where, after rain,
Salamanders lay, looped the dark moss with gold.
High up, in a glade,
Bells clanged, the cowherd boy
Was carving a pipe.

And I moved on, to learn
One of the million histories,
One weather, one dialect
Of herbs, one habitat
After migration, displacement,
With greedy lore to pounce
On a place and possess it,
With the mind's weapons, words,
While between land and water
Yellow vultures, mewing,
Looped empty air
Once filled with the hundred names
Of the nameless, or swooped
To the rocks, for carrion.

2

Enough now, of grabbing, holding,
The wars fought for peace,
Great loads of equipment lugged
To the borders of bogland, dumped,
So that empty-handed, empty-minded,
A few stragglers could stagger home.

And my baggage – those tags, the stickers
That brag of a Grand Hotel
Requisitioned for troops, then demolished,
Of a tropical island converted
Into a golf course;
The specimens, photographs, notes –
The heavier it grew, the less it was needed,
The longer it strayed, misdirected,
The less it was missed.

3

Mountains. A lake.
One of a famous number.
I see these birds, they dip over wavelets,
Looping, martins or swallows,
Their flight is enough.
The lake is enough,
To be here, forgetful,
In a boat, on water.
The famous dead have been here.
They saw and named what I see,
They went and forgot.

I climb a mountainside, soggy.
Then springy with heather.
The clouds are low,
The shaggy sheep have a name,
Old, less old than the breed
Less old than the rock
And I smell hot thyme
That grows in another country,
Through gaps in the Roman wall
A cold wind carries it here,

4

Through gaps in the mind,
Its fortifications, names:
Name that a Roman gave
To a camp on the moor
Where a sheep's jawbone lies
And buzzards, mewing, loop
Air between woods and water
Long empty of his gods;

Name of the yellow poppy
Drooping, after rain,
Or the flash, golden,
From wings in flight –
Greenfinch or yellowhammer –

Of this mountain, this lake. I move on.

V

1

Now or before, when the dogwood flowered
And you came walking out of no street or house
Known to me, with a gift
So much more than itself that the promise
Could not be kept. But the loan
Was mine, to consume like the air
Of that 'sweete and most healthfullest climate',
Yours while you walk there, changed,
Breathing its loan of air,
And the dogwood flowers
Where other trees grew,
'Great, tall, soft, light,
And yet tough enough I think to be fitte
Also for masts of shippes'
Of the kind sunk by sandbanks,
Battered by hurricanes there,
At the wild cape.

Gone, lost, the trees and the ships,
The possession and hope of possession;
Found, through the giving up,
Where I'm not, on the white sands,
A shell in her hand, she, 'for ever fair'.

2

I move on, closer now to the end
That is no end as long as
One mountain remains, one lake,
One river, one forest
Yet to be named, possessed,
Relinquished, forgotten, left
For Earth to renew. Move on
To no end but of 'I', 'you'
And the linking words, love's

Though love has no end,
Though words, when the link is broken,
Move on beyond 'I' and 'you',

3

As do his, who forsook the place,
His traffic island where love
Set up house and raised orphans,
Tenderly taught them to till
The hardest rock. Yet, after so much,
Gave in, to his blood's revolt
Against veins, against the heart
Pushing its dope, pumping
And pumping hope
Out into limbs that had learnt,
From things touched, to be still.
Could not eat now, the new bread
That tasted of flesh left unburied
Decades, frontiers ago,
Could not drink now, the new wine
That tasted of salt,
From a dry sea,
From a blinded eye,
And, slowly, began to go
Where he must, where
His poems had gone before him,
Into silence now, silence,
Water at last, water
Which, unclean, could wash
All it flows over, fills,
Even his mouth, of last words,
And move on.

4

Slowly, detained by love,
He went, but never
Slowly enough for Earth
In her long slow dream

That has not finished yet
With the gestation of man,
The breaker of her dream,
And has not finished
Digesting the teeth and bones
Of her dinosaurs.

Making and breaking words,
For slowness,
He opened gaps, for a pulse
Less awake, less impatient
Than his, who longed
To be dreamed again,
Out of pulverized rock,
Out of humus,
Bones, anthropoid, saurian,
And the plumage of orioles;
Cleared a space, for the poems
That Earth might compose
'On the other side
Of mankind'
And our quick ears
Could not hear.

5

Gone. Lost. Half-forgotten already
What quick eyes took in,
Quick hands felt the shape of, tongue
Touched with a name. Half-forgotten
The oriole's drab call
High up, on the crest of a flowering pear-tree,
A month or two back, not here,
Not in the city garden
Where from a drabber throat
A thrush luxuriantly warbles and foxgloves
Find a wood, though the woods were felled.

IX

1

Together we've walked, and apart,
Over mountains, by lakes,
On sea shores, of sand, pebble, rock,
Moorland or marshland, on cliffs
Overgrown or sheer, through woods
Dark with leafage or dense
With bramble, scrub, bracken;
Down streets of how many cities,
On cobbles, on brick, on slabs
Always dabbed with old blood or new;
To look, to listen, to take in
And discard the dialects, histories,
To discover, uncover, a bareness
More lastingly ours; to return
And, dying a little, become
Less than we were, and more
By the loss, by the giving back;
If not moving, moved on,
Out of ourselves, beyond
'I', "you", and there
Brought to a meeting again
After difference, barer;
Hardly daring to speak
The other's name or the word
Of sameness in otherness, love;

2

To name a thing or a place,
Lest the name stick to a husk,
To a stump, to the gateway left
When a house was demolished.
                              No,
Let the light record it, the seedling
That rises once more to the light
Where the parent's taproot was cut;

Or love's element only,
Fire, the last and first –
Let it blast, consume, reduce,
Propel, transmute; and create
Again, out of glowing rock-mash, an island,
Out of loose, mad atoms a planet.

3

For a while, though, yet
It's the wind, the sky's colour
That will bring us news. Today
Blackish clouds, blown, merge
And fray; their shadows race
Along pavement, lawn, chasing
Break-away sunbeams. A hint
Of hyacinth now; stronger,
The odour of soil roused
By showers, with last year's leaves
And wood-ash being rendered,
Washed down, mixed in, still,

4

Whether or not we see them, mountains, lakes,
The forgotten, the unknown, breathing
Heather or thyme, blossom of lemon or laurel,
Pine tang, salt tang or tar or dust;
Trusting the name, seek out
A roadside changed, grown strange,
Or await the turn and recurrence
Of mind's, of blood's weather,
Fragrances that a breeze
Blew where we walked, blew beyond us
And blows to someone, to no one;
Stop here, move on.

In Suffolk I

1

So many moods of light, sky,
Such a flux of cloud shapes,
Cloud colours blending, blurring,
And the winds, to be learnt by heart:
So much movement to make a staying.

So much labour, with no time for looking,
Before trees wrenched free of ivy
Behind lowered eyelids began
To be ash or alder or willow.

So much delving down
With fork, spade, bare hands
To endangered roots before,
Weighed, breathed in, this earth
Made known its manyness
Of sand, humus, loam,
Of saturation, and so
Began to permit a tenure.

2

Landscape? Not yet. Even now,
Though more than a year of weathers
Has rushed, crept through the trees,
Leaved, stripped, torn off
Old boughs, snapped
Trunks of the newly planted.
In its burgeoning froze
This young medlar? Bending it,
Ripped the fine roots?
Other weathers will tell;

Let a dark red glow perhaps
Come again from the copper beech
Through translucent foliage, in May;
Deepen again the blackness
Of conifer woods, and pierce it.

Later perhaps, out of changing shapes,
A landscape will seem to grow,
Seem to cohere: a system
Of marsh and heath, of meadow
And forest, all veined
With waterways, roads. Not yet.

3

Winter. A night long
Gales tried the house. Rain
Found a way in. A gutter's
Jagged end hangs loose.
Iron sheets from a roof
Jam the holly hedge.
A telephone pole
Bars the lane to the village.

But bright the eastern sky
Breaks. Blue rivulets
Streak the grey north.
Mild or harsh, the day
Will be only itself.

4

Snow brings in snipe
To the sodden lawn
Pocked with molehills. Their bills
Jerk, prodding by inches
Down to the mud between clumps.
Now a tomcat prowls
The verge. They cower,
Motionless, merge in the cleared ruts.

Fieldfare alights, to fight
With blackbird, song thrush
Till a gull swoops down,
Then a jackdaw, to rob them and fight.
Only a lapwing keeps aloof,
Stalks at the far end.

5

Sunshine, a quick thaw.
And all are gone. A gust,
And even the sparrows, robins
Are not to be seen or heard;
But in the distance, wind-blurred,
Lapwing's, gull's cry.

VIII

1

Brooding light. The days muted,
Muffled, as though no noise
From fighter 'plane, truck,
No voice from village or pasture
Could pierce it, this wad of silence
The land's put on; no wind,
Ruffling leafage still thick,
Green or yellowing (silvery
White, upturned, on the poplars)
Could prod a tree to hurry
Over the business of fall.

2

Though as ever the air flows,
Freely grass and weeds
Grow, from new seed
Recently scattered, a circle,
Somewhere, is full, as the barns are,
The next not yet begun.

Michaelmas. Season
Of seasonless blossoming,
Ghostly; termination
Of tenure; removal; repair.

Silent through mat silken skies,
High up, the last martins glided,
Swallows and swifts gone.
From reedbeds and shores now
Slower wings flap,
Black arrowhead, to the south.

Dubiously day breaks.
A glimmer creeps into low haze
With the moon bright above it,
One star bright and the hinted flicker
Of other stars, too faint,
Too far for the eye's habit.

No thrush responds to such dawning.
Far off, a cock's crow, faint,
Merges in cattle's lowing
And is drowned in a bellow, a wail
That seems to slide up from the doom
Of their patient, their used kind,
Though a call merely, for milking.
Yet the stillness holds, stronger.

4

Towards mid-morning, a second dawn
As the sun breaks through, warm
Between black cloud-drifts;
But an introversion of earth
Leaves the day suspended.
Late flowers, late fruit obey
No urge but their own to linger,
Dismissed by the year's waning,
Fill a time all their own,
All aftermath, hushed;

And are most themselves in the half-hour
When even the damped shine
Begins to fade, their colours
Owe least to light's collusion,
Their glowing a cold fire
Kindled, fed from within.

The eye it is, wearying
After pale pinks and mauves,
Ghostly, of colchicum,
Michaelmas daisy, that bleeds
Last poppies of their scarlet.

The mind it is that withdraws
Into a winter, impatient
Not only for rest but the buds
On boughs not yet leafless;
Bent on its own rebirth,
Finds this dying too slow,
Leaps from fruition, store
To its greater need, hope,

To digging once more, in grey drizzle,
To sowing once more the turned earth,
While still the ungathered apples are gathering sunrays
On the tops of tall trees, and quinces deepening
Their lime to downed lemon, their lemon to gold.

IX

1

Winter solstice. Air
Takes over from earth at rest.
A hawk braves the gale,
Hangs over stalks that snap
Or fold at the base, mouldy.

Sky takes over, from land,
At sunrise, sundown bursts
Into a cold fluorescence,
As though all the brightness lost
To beech leaves that, withered,
Russet, remain unfallen,
To ilex, holly, fir,
And a year's whole range of blossom
Had gathered up there, to shine.

Here, only water
Responds to such light;
And fire holds its own.
If a kingfisher now
Flashed, cock pheasant
Nodded by, near,
At noon, yet they would fade
And eyes be referred higher.

2

Only in windless nights,
Damp, without frost,
By starlight a haze dims,
Still earth emits
Hints of growth in decay,
Cattle smell, care
And hope, smell of straw,
Hay, of wood smoke,

Rising too, drifting
Away, exhaled by fire
Into air, leaving
White ashes only
To be mixed back into earth
By water, and feed roots.

3

When heavy wings beat
In slow time, silent,
Trace the river-banks,
Measure a heavier stillness
And close, merged in mist,
A thin line, vanishing,
It is a heron between
Earth and water and air,

Effigy now of a bird,
Or signpost, fixed, that points
Out of its world and ours
Into blankness, extinction:
Blasting of all the ways,
All the kinds and weathers
By deadly fire, fission.

4

And in dim light on the village green
Round the tall spruce hung
With electric bulbs, in a broken circle
Faltering singers fumbled
For words that seemed half-forgotten,
Unable to rise against
Darkness not dark enough,
Silence not silent enough,

Since a loudspeaker purveyed
The finished product, sweetened
With a cinema organ's falsetto,
A confection of tinkling bells,
And prompted nothing, but shamed back
Into half-silence their voices,
Into half-darkness their hope,

Till the ceremony had ceased,
Till the words were not summoned,
Till out of the circle of light
Each walked back lonelier
Under the same star
To a house less owned.

5

For the moment, breathing clean air
That tastes new, renewed like the year,
The decade soon to begin, they look up
To the same star, can hear the words
Left unsaid, unsung, a music more quiet
Yet harsher, remember the hope put away,
The remedy kept in reserve and passed on
Heart to heart, with a whispered warning:
For external use only. Danger.
Can be fatal if taken internally,
Applied in excess or in the wrong place;

And, recurrent too, a dread
That the promise could be fulfilled,
The time near when truth
Is exacted whole, stark:
No spring after winter,
No growth from any sowing,
All ways, all weathers blighted,
And only in them, the unhoused,
As earth and sky break,
That love at last, burning.

Dream Poems

The Road

It begins near Venice,
A Venice of chasms and pools,
And above a coastline longer than vision
Gently curves
Into a south or east without end.
Always the question is
How far can I walk it
Across what frontiers
Into what vastnesses,
More golden mist,
Woods even denser, darker,
Mountains more mountainous
Above a more dazzling sea.

Always I am detained;
As by this new nation
Of displaced persons
Who are rarely visited,
Whose nationhood is a cause.
They needed me,
Appealed to my friendship,
Involved me in schemes,
Charged me with missions
To friends whom I never reached.

If only I could move on
To the wilder, more alien countries
Farther along the road.

The Search

As commanded, I looked for my origin,
Passed through the town in which my grandfather settled
And found no street that I knew;
On through the suburbs, blind bungalows,
Lilac, laburnum, narrowly flowering
And out into mountains, woods,
Far provinces, infinities of green.
Walked, walked, by day, by night,
Always sure of the route
Though the people grew foreign, bizarre;
And the birds, a species unheard of, remembered me.
At last I came to a village
Where they told me: here you were born.
An unlikely place – no petrol pump, office block, poster? –
Yet I could not deny it, and asked them the name.
Why, Mors, need we tell you, m o r s, MORS.

For No One

So we meet again, little girl
Whose blue eyes taught me
How to say nothing, to look
And be merged in looking.
I saw you there and I listened,
But you cannot hear me,
Nor do I know where you are.
No need, in that place
Where to look is enough,
Where to meet is a marriage
Nowhere, for ever,
Nothing can be undone.

Here, I should have passed by, unrecognizing,
You a woman now, still young but not beautiful,
With a bad complexion. But Beatrice was your name,
Recalled to me without words though your eyes were not even
    blue
And now you chattered gaily about yourself,
About living from hand to mouth, luxuriously.
Because you were Beatrice, nothing had changed between us;
Because nothing had changed between us, I knew your name.

Memory

My wives do not write.
Sweetly young, hair flowing,
They walk where they belong,
Riverside, lakeside,
Mountainside, hillside,
Woodland or grassy plain.

One I consoled –
Black-haired, sad
In her forest clearing –
Another I followed
From a wellspring up in the scree
To a pool's golden rushes.

Did I leave them, forsake them?
I travelled,
Remember no parting.
Ways, I recall, transitions,
The shadows, the colours turning,
Herbs acrid or heady,
Sweet wives the world over,
Sweet virgins walking where they belong –

Unchanged, unchanging regions,
And they unchanged.

But by the knee a stranger
Clawed me, held on;
I fought: my grappling hand
Slid deep into rotten flesh,
A hole behind his ear.
I knocked him down and ran,
Clegs covering me,
A grey crust;
Ran to the church, thinking
They could not enter there,
But still they clung, stinging,
And up I climbed, climbed

To the belfry, pursued
By a man half-decayed.

Sweet wives, sweet virgins
Walk still unchanged,
Do not write, do not miss me,
Never forget.
It was the sunshine, the shadows,
It was the herbs and the haze.

The Blight

Somewhere behind us, from the long room,
Sear-frost, look! cried a child's voice
As fingertips touching we stood
At the window and looked,
Felt the sap run again
From the root up,
New boughs burgeon under the new sun.

Sear-frost, in April?
There it was, icy rain,
And the leaves turned black, curled,
Bud, blossom shrivelled, fell,
Not one year's growth but the whole tree withered.

Your hand froze in mine,
Froze mine, yet tightened, the nails
Dug in through flesh drained numb,
Dug down to the bones and a deep nerve.

Let go, if you can.

Too slowly toward the root
Our death creeps.

Theogony

One feather, scarlet, on snow:
High rose the bird
That feeds by winter moonlight,
Warbles on farthest mountain tops,
By no man snared, by no man plucked or eaten.

One golden hair
Found on the pillow:
The woman gone, Diana of all that was hers
Grazes with absence the tiled floor
And hallows it, touched by her feet once.

Dream Houses I

They have a history, dream history
Of how acquired, when occupied
And why vacated, those haunted half-ruins
Inherited only from earlier dreams,
Half-obscured by a wilderness
That once was garden or park.

The precise location, boundaries
Are dubious, as are my rights
Of freehold, leasehold, mere lodging.
For strangers have moved in,
Families, communes, beside
Those nearest to me
Now or at any time,
She who left me, she whom I left,
He whose handwriting changed, he whom frustration bent,
Each with a choice between many faces,
Youthful or aging, never estranged;
And the dead cohabit there with the living.

Yet the great hall, higher than warehouse, chapel,
Hidden behind the façade, reached
By going down – a staircase wide, bright,
Not winding – remains inaccessible,
Because unknown, to the newer tenants.
That hall, the alluring extension
Of one house alone, is the heart of them all.
Its bare walls, floor of grey stone
Untouched by furniture, offer
Pure luxury, space
Enclosed, held, not by me,
To immure a silence,

home.

An emptiness?

There they are,
Invisible, the living, the dead,
In a house inhabited once
And mislaid like a letter giving
Details, dates, movements
That could consummate love.

Every meeting is there,
Every parting, the word
Hardly whispered, more sensed
Than heard: all retained by the bare walls
Of the hidden hall in the tall house
Mine and not mine.

Outside,
Where trees tower, meadows and heathland merge
In the foothills of high ranges,
The laughter of children hovers,
This muffled hammerbeat
Is their murdered great-grandmother, walking.

Dream Houses II

1

Deep down, underneath a cellar
Lay the remains of a corpse
Hidden there – with whose help? –
After a killing I had not willed
Yet had done – or never done? –
That had happened, in horror,
Revulsion, remorse at the doing,
Fear less of punishment
Than of the thing done, the knowledge
That unwilled it was done
By hands mine and not mine –
So long ago, I could nearly doubt it.

2

Into the house now – which house? –
My father, the doctor, has moved
From his death; and, let into the secret
By no doer, no helper, no spy,
Without one word, applies himself
To the deed's undoing, the resurrection
Of a bundle of stinking bones.
On to a bed he's carried it; and sits
On the edge, bends over it
Till by attention, care, he's infused
A breath that forms flesh.

3

So that was the victim – I had forgotten.
She's risen, she walks, an elderly lady,
Benign, and remembers no murder,
A guest in the house. She could leave.
Let her stay. For the staying proves
That our house is healthy now, healed
(That I am healed of the horror,
The deed done, never done).

4

Then the house cracked. (It was one left
Long ago, in the war, and demolished.)
As I washed my hands I heard
Bricks fall, and felt,
Deep down, a swaying, a sliding
Of beams. But trusted them still.
The floor I stood on held,
Water still flowed from the tap.

153

5

My life's houses are one,
The lived in, the left, the levelled.
In a lost garden, though,
Roses are flowering, in winter,
The leafage is lush.
In another I look for my children
And all my children are gone.
Ploughed fields, brown marshes
Up to the long horizon;
A lapwing flying.
Not a sound from the house.
Not a sound in the air.

Night . . .

Night. A man clears a border, throwing
Plucked weeds, broken-off twigs of shrubs
Forward, against the wall of his house, against
That in the air which whispers: so late, so late.
Delinquent hands. Delinquency of hands
Driven to impose an order still on rankness
When, our own order lost, we are less than grass.
Labours in drum-taut stillness, pauses, and hears
Mated shrieks of barnowl and moorhen,
Vixen and leveret in the one dark's grip;
Knowing: lostness it is that keeps me, that holds me here.
Till another cry rips him, his own name
Called out again and again, in the house,
By her his absence has woken, who looks for him now,
Whom, so near, so near, he can summon no voice to answer,
No motion to comfort, his feet leaden with loss.

In No Time

A drifting it was, as though back into youth
But more free and easy, this terminal party
Thrown by no visible host, with couples
Forming and breaking up in no time
(In no time the party took place, at no place
Anyone there could have named or remembered.)
And he, adrift, almost at once had been drawn
To a dark-eyed woman with pale hair,
Talked with her, drifted off again towards others,
Seeing her deeply engaged with another man,
But she returned to him, closer to him than before,
And their talk flowed like one river's water,
Now eddying, rushing, now stalled in pools that look still
Over a bed so ancient, to them it seemed changeless.

Together they left, as one, their wishes, their thoughts
Wedded in no time (for time
Was about to end, to no end
They or anyone could have named,
No one will live to remember),
And by no audible word of command were drawn
Or driven into a garden –
His once, he told her – that was to be stripped, they knew,
Of all that grew there, species, hybrid or graft,
Down to the bare black soil, up to the branches,
Beyond their reach, of overshadowing trees.
(For light and the colours light played on for eyes
That colluded with light, with colours, would now be put out
And the eyes put out in no time.)

Worked, as one, towards the garden's unmaking,
Towards their own, so that bare as the black soil
They would be one indeed at the consummation,
Wholly in body and mind would share
Their every possession, none.

And the weather sickened, disowning the season,
Swallows hurtled and crashed as the air-streams collided,
The trees, together, shook off all their blight of leaves
On to them who, melting, dissolved in each other,
Were blind in no time, at one with their world.

Dying

So that's what it's like: hearing them talk still
In a whisper, and letting your love pick up
Crumbs in response from the bare table
Till – there are crumbs left, things to be said
And their voices are audible still and their faces
Clearer than ever – another need
Orders withdrawal, silence.
A bad joke, you think, this pretending not to be there –
And are gone, where they will follow.
Going, have punctured the bubble, time,
So that your wide-open eyes insist:
Speak louder, my near ones, laugh, and rejoice.

On Duty

Attending the telephone
I take to be still connected
To some headquarters or other
Become expert in reticence,
I try to remember the old war
I joined up for, but can't get beyond
The trestle bed I rose from
This morning, any morning,
In a barrack room shared with no one;
And can't be sure when it was
That a bugle inside my head,
Blowing reveille, became
The blare that roused me from nightmare
At the moment of sudden awareness
That years or decades have passed
Since my parents answered a letter,
Of the flash in darkness showing me
The girl I was to have married
Smile to herself undecided
Between two bedroom doors,
Each with a man behind it.
Awake, must ask myself,
Man? Is the designation current?
If ever again a voice
Should come through, will it use
Human, obsolete words
To charge, discharge me
Whose number, rank, name
Were dropped long ago
From records transferred to computers,
And leave this table real,
This pen, the blank forms?

Or is silence not only the code
But the message I'm here to receive
And pass on, undeciphered?
Pass on to whom, though, to whom?

Endless

It began as a couch grass root,
Stringy and white,
Straggling, to no end,
Branching out, breaking
For procreation.

Traced and pulled, it became
A bramble shoot that climbed
Through leafage of shrub, tree
With a root at its tip, for plunging.

I pulled at it, pulled,
Miles of the thing came away,
More and more.

I pulled and pulled until
I saw that now
Straight up it had risen
With its end in space,
With a root in heaven.

Recovery

To swim I had gone out,
Towards noon, in hot weather.

With four diseases, my clothes mislaid or stolen,
By nightfall I crawled the streets.

If I lay low, I was done for.
If I showed myself, naked, what then?

There was this rag of towel
And I could not give in.

From behind dustbins, skips,
I dragged myself to a door –

Of a shed, it seemed, workshop or store,
For directions at best, mediation.

The woman laughed, but she let me in.
I looked, and the place was a ward.

"It's made up, for you", she said,
Laughing still, pointing

To the first bed on the right.
"You'll need no loincloth here.

Nor more rest than it takes to tell
Which illness is that you'd have died of.

By then there'll be light again
For you to go home by, healed."